Sally,
you are such a wonderful
person, thank you for a
your support. Best W
in all of your endeavors, I
know you will succeed

Eva Marie

Letters
To My
Husband's
Mistress

Letters To My Husband's Mistress

Eva-Marie

The author has tried to recreate events, locations, and conversations from her memories of them. In some instances, in order to maintain their anonymity, the author has changed the names of individuals and places. she may also have changed some identifying characteristics and details such as physical attributes, occupations, and places of residence.

ISBN: 978-0-9963508-0-8

10 9 8 7 6 5 4 3 2   0 4 2 7 1 5

Printed in the United States of America

∞This paper meets the requirements of ANSI/NISO Z39.48-1992 (Permanence of Paper)

In memory of my beloved parents,
who instilled great morals and values in my life.

Table of Contents

Acknowledgments

The deepest, most heartfelt expression of gratitude goes to my four wonderful children, who, in spite of experiencing their own pain and turmoil at the time, did everything in their power to make sure that we remained a close family and supported each other. I want to thank my son-in-law, who has really been more like a son in every way possible, and my grandkids who supplied an abundance of love.

I want to take this opportunity to also say a huge thank you to my wonderful siblings, in-laws from both my siblings and my ex-husband, and my numerous nieces and nephews. I cannot forget to mention my amazing friends and professional associates as well. Everyone in my life stood on the sidelines and cheered me on. I assure you I would not be where I am today had it not been for the love and support of every one of my family members and friends. I consider each and every one of you to be the blessings in my life and the wind beneath my wings. You all gave me the strength to get out of bed every day and be productive. At no time during my ordeal did I ever feel that I was alone. All that I have accomplished, since my life had the sudden change of direction, I credit to my family and friends, who were determined to see me become victorious in spite of life's vicissitudes.

My gratitude is also extended to my therapist and friend; my doctor who managed all the health issues I developed during this time; my professor at my university who helped me to see myself as an inspiration to others; my friend and attorney who assisted me in the early stages in my divorce; my friend, Romeo, who helped me with most matters pertaining to mine and my daughter's vehicle and became a truly good friend in the process; my friend Gary for helping me with numerous problems related to household and computer repairs; Dionne, for being so wonderful to me in many ways, but most importantly, she typed my book once it was written; and Debbie Lawrence, the author of *Your Year of Turn Around: Forty Days of Encouragement*, who was my inspiration and became my self-appointed coach, mentor, and motivator.

Introduction

Matthew 19:4–6: He answered, "Have you not read that he who created them from the beginning made them male and female, and said, 'Therefore a man shall leave his father and his mother and hold fast to his wife, and the two shall become one flesh'? So they are no longer two but one flesh. What therefore God has joined together, let not man separate."

The sixth commandment: "Thou shalt not commit adultery."

The ninth commandment: "Thou shalt not covet your neighbor's wife"

Most people reading this book right now are familiar with at least one or all three of the above biblical quotes.

Judging by the immorality explosion taking place in our society right now, it makes me ask the question, does anyone care what is said in the Bible?

I embarked on this project of writing my book and telling my story for several reasons.

1. Infidelity is wrong and it does not matter how long it has been around and how many people are doing it; it is painful and destructive.

2. In today's society, cheating seems to have become a sport and the participants seem to have no shame.

3. The world is really in a sad place when women who are mistresses are

   A. proud and unashamed of their position as a mistress.

   B. given the forum on live television programs to speak about themselves and their adulterous relationships. Some even write books and speak negatively about the wife of their married lover; how sad!

We are all privy to information about Tiger Woods and his multitude of mistresses, John Edwards and Rielle Hunter, Arnold Schwarzenegger and his nanny, Bill Clinton and Monica Lewinsky, Elliott Spitzer and Ashley Dupree, just to name a few. The sad situation behind all these affairs is that there are wives and children. No one ever hears about them. They are the silent victims of infidelity who are never given an opportunity to express their pain and explain to all the women out there who think it is acceptable to sleep with a married man what their immorality has done and what pain it has caused.

I was with my husband for thirty-nine years at the time of my divorce and married for thirty-six. It goes to show that no one is immune or exempt from infidelity no matter how long you were married.

I want to tell my story to be the voice for all those women who have walked in my shoes, whether your marriage survived the affair or not. I want women to know that there is life after an affair or a divorce. I want to tell my story so I can be of some support to women and children who are the victims of cheating husbands and their mistresses. Wives, do not be ashamed. You have done nothing wrong. My husband's mistress fought me for my husband with the help of her family, my husband's boss, and a campaign of harassment executed by her sister. The sad thing is that both my ex-husband and his mistress/wife are living a lie, giving the world the impression that their marriage was built on love. Well, my children, my family, my friends and I are here to let the world know that their marriage was built on other people's pain. I want my ex-husband and his mistress/wife and their family to know everything about what pain they caused my children and I and the truth about the lie they are living.

Part I

In the Beginning

Dear Mistress Ali,

At a farewell party held in my honor, I was introduced to this tall skinny guy by my neighbor, Ernest, who was the DJ of the party. The tall skinny guy was his friend. I was seventeen years old and migrating to the United States with my mother. My dad was to join us in a few months. That was a very sad time in my life as I was leaving all my friends one year before graduating from high school and migrating to a new country to begin at a new school in a new country, new home, to meet new friends and to enter into a whole new culture. It was overwhelming, to say the least. At the party, I danced with the tall guy a couple of times, but nothing was memorable about him other than the fact that he had on a blue shirt. He was so tall it hurt

3

my neck to dance with him. My real memories of that night were being with all my friends and having fun.

One year later, I returned to my homeland to attend and be a part of my friends' graduation party. My best friend, Hannah, was attending the party with my friend, neighbor, and DJ from my farewell party, Ernest. Upon realizing that he would be attending the party with both girls, I think Ernest thought three's a crowd, so he quickly made contact with his friend, the tall skinny guy whose name was Dan, and invited him to the graduation party. We all had a lot of fun at the party, but I had the best time of all being reunited with all of my high school friends whom I had kept in touch with by writing letters every day for the entire year that I was in the United States. Being at that graduation party had me in a state of complete euphoria, in contrast to my twelfth grade year, which I spent in a new school, in a new culture, where I felt lonely and isolated.

I stayed in Trinidad for two and a half weeks after the graduation party and found myself in the company of Dan every day for the duration of my vacation. My neighbor Ernest was dating my friend Hannah who, according to her parents, was not allowed to date. However, her parents approved of our friendship, and as a result, had no problem with Hannah spending the entire three weeks with me while I was in Trinidad on vacation. Neither Hannah nor I felt it was okay for her to go out with Ernest alone, so I tagged along. Ernest had no intentions of having me along every time he ventured out on a date with my friend, so he decided to bring along his friend to keep me occupied while he walked on the beach, danced in the club, or attended the movies with Hannah alone. Dan was forced to interact with me, and I with him. We talked and laughed together and often found humor in the fact that we were not dating but we were together every day at every place that Ernest and Hannah went on their date. The more time Dan and I spent together, the more we talked and the more interesting he became, and pretty soon the words *tall* and *skinny* were replaced with *handsome* and *sweet*.

During the course of our many conversations, I learned that sweet, handsome Dan was migrating to the United States the following month. The prospect of continuing our friendship when he came to the United States was very exciting to me, and apparently it was to him also, because the night before I left to return home to the US Dan told me that he would love to continue seeing me when he comes to the US and made me laugh when he said, "Thank God this time it would be voluntary and without Ernest and Hannah." I was really excited at that thought and we exchanged phone numbers.

The very day Dan arrived in the US, he called me and we began dating the following week. We spoke on the phone daily for hours and saw each other as often as we could. We quickly became best friends and really enjoyed each other's company. At the time, Dan lived in the Bronx and I lived in Brooklyn. Dan did not have a car at the time, so riding the New York subway was his mode of transportation. That did not stop him from visiting me every week when he was off from work.

Dan was the guy I'd been dreaming of. He was caring, thoughtful, very romantic, and treated me like a queen. Because of Dan's easygoing disposition, he quickly became close friends with my brother Allen. Many times my brother would allow him to stay overnight at his home instead of getting on the subway after one of our dates. I was happy about that because I always felt a bit guilty. After our dates, he would take me home and then he had to make a two-hour commute to go to his home in the Bronx. As a result of my brother's kindness toward Dan, they established a close friendship that lasted a bit longer than my marriage. About one year after dating, Dan and I were madly in love and we began to talk about spending the rest of our lives together. We became officially engaged two and a half years later on December 31, 1974. We were married three years and one month after the day we met on July 26, 1975. (Ernest and Hannah both married different people.)

My wedding was quite a spectacular affair, with family and friends coming from everywhere to be part of the celebration. Our marriage was blessed by both our parents. I loved Dan's family and they loved me. His mother was the best mother-in-law any girl could have hoped for. His sisters and brothers were wonderful to me. I was happy and in love. I was not only loved by my husband, but also by his entire family. Dan also loved and respected my parents and siblings. Everyone in my family loved Dan as well. Because Dan and I dated for three years and one month before we tied the knot, close relationships between himself and my family members were formed long before our wedding. My parents, whom I loved and respected more than anything, were very happy with my choice of husband. My two older brothers, who were very protective of their sister, not only loved Dan but also thought of him as a brother before we were even married. My oldest brother, who still considered me to be his baby sister, was a little more resistant to that brotherly love so early in the friendship. Dan made no special effort to win him over, but it was not long before my oldest brother accepted him into our family without any reservations.

As newlyweds do, Dan and I made plans together about our future. I had taken a medical leave of absence from college in my freshman year and Dan started at a different college around the same time. As we were now a married couple, we decided that it wouldn't make much sense for both of us to work and attend school at the same time. It would make more sense for him to work and go to school and I would just work until he graduated. Then, I would go to school and he would work, assuming that upon graduation he would have been in a position to secure a much better paying job. Well, my mother always said, "If you want to hear God laugh, make a plan." That statement was so apropos. On May 25, 1977, the day of Dan's final exam before graduation, our precious son Nick was born. To say that Dan and I were ecstatic would be an understatement. Fortunately, my pregnancy was what I defined as a great experience. I was not sick, not one day in the entire nine months, and was fortunate to have been able to continue working until just one week before our son was born.

Fifteen months later, Dan had still not found that "better paying job" and I was then pregnant with our second child. Dan had been working two jobs in order to support his family. At times he became a bit frustrated and tired of the routine, but we prayed every day that the job he was so desperately seeking would be found. With a nineteen-month-old baby and another on the way, we decided to take a trip to Trinidad while we still could to visit our friends and family for Christmas. This trip changed our lives in a way that we could not have expected or anticipated. While in Trinidad, thanks to a friend, Dan was offered a job with a very lucrative compensation package. He accepted the job. Needless to say, at this point all my plans of returning to college to complete my degree were now derailed.

Dan returned to the US in January to shop, pack, and ship our household belongings. He worked for a couple more months, resigned both his jobs, and returned to Trinidad in time for our baby's arrival, which was met with as much excitement and joy as our firstborn's, though neither of us thought that was possible. On May 17, 1979, we welcomed our precious, beautiful baby girl Simone.

Dan and I continued to reside in Trinidad for another seven years, during which time we gave birth to Kyle, born on July 17, 1984, another one of God's gifts. When Kyle was two years old, there was a drastic change in the economy in Trinidad and Tobago. Dan's mom and some of his siblings were living in the US, so we made a decision to return there. Dan had been working at a very demanding job in Trinidad where he gained a wealth of knowledge and experience and decided to give the US job market one more try. Seven years after living in Trinidad, we migrated to Queens, New York. We lived in New York for one short year.

The transition was a difficult one for each of us, but we got through it as a family. Dan and I shared the same priorities, which were our children. We did whatever worked for them; no matter the sacrifice, we worked as a team. We were fortunate to attain employment with Pan Am Airlines shortly after we found an apartment. I worked from 6:00 a.m. to 10:00 a.m. and Dan worked from 9:00 a.m. until 5:00 p.m. We made a decision to put our two older children in Catholic school to help with their adjustment because that's what they were accustomed to in Trinidad. Needless to say, it was quite expensive to have one child in nursery school and two children in Catholic school. The money we were making was just not enough. Since I only worked a few hours at Pan Am, we decided and agreed that I should get another job.

I got another job, working from 7:00 p.m. until 3:00 a.m. That was not easy, but it was necessary. I left to go to work at 6:00 p.m. and came home at 3:45 a.m., then left for my other job at 5:15 a.m. and returned home at 10:30 a.m. I would sleep for about four hours and then go pick up the children from school. Once we came home, I prepared dinner and we ate before I had to leave for work again at 6:00 p.m. Dan took care of the kids' afterschool and bedtime routine, laundry, and cleaned up after dinner. I never complained, and neither did he. We just did what it took. It was no different from when we were first married and Dan worked full-time and attended university full-time as well.

After one year of this routine, Dan decided that he wanted to move to Atlanta, but I wanted to move to Florida, where all my siblings were living. In July, we took a weekend trip to Atlanta for our anniversary. By the end of the three-day visit to Atlanta, I was sold on the idea of moving there too. I got a transfer with Pan Am, and by August the children and I were living in Atlanta so that they could start the school year. Dan found a job and moved in November that year.

When we moved to Atlanta and gave birth to our fourth child, Mia, Dan did not want me to work. Apart from his nine- to-five, he had a part-time job on evenings and weekends. With four children, two jobs just afforded us the ability to pay our bills and feed and clothe ourselves and our children. Neither of us complained as we always tried to make life easier for one another. We had dinner as a family every night before Dan left for his part-time job. When it came to disciplining the kids, we supported each other in front of the kids even though we may have disagreed behind closed doors. Dan was pretty strict with the boys but much more lenient with the girls. I cooked. Dan cooked. I did laundry. Dan did laundry. I cleaned. Dan cleaned. We both loved to entertain. When the kids were younger, both Dan and I shared the household responsibilities; not necessarily 50/50, but fair enough. I did not share the financial responsibility 50/50 either, but it was also fair enough.

When my last daughter started school in 1995, I went back out to work. Dan did not like the idea, but we made it work for a while. Dan was not the one in our relationship that had the responsibility of the children's school activities and academic progress. An example of this was when Mia started school. Dan had the job of getting her registered as I had just started a new job. About two weeks after school began, I took Mia to school and wanted to meet her teacher.

While walking toward the kindergarten hall with Mia to go to her class, she kept saying, "This is not the way to my class."

I ignored her. When we actually got to the kindergarten hall I asked, "Which classroom is yours?"

Again she said, "This is not the way to my class."

Bewildered at this point, I instructed her to take me to her class. Upon arriving, I saw written in big letters on the wall next to the door "First Grade." I walked in and introduced myself to the teacher, who expressed her pleasure to meet me and continued to let me know that she was going to give me a call sometime that week, her reason being that all of the rosters were finally complete and Mia's name was not on hers. Just to be 100 percent sure I asked what grade this was and she told me first. I had to explain to the teacher that my husband was the one who registered Mia. Clearly he was out of his league in this area and had no idea what he was doing. Mia turned five the very week school opened in August, but when he registered her he put her in first grade. We were both amused by this incident, and the teacher even suggested Mia remain in first grade because she was academically on level with the other children in the class. I did not choose that option as Mia was still my baby, who just turned five and needed to be with the babies in kindergarten.

By the end of the first term in December of that year, I withdrew Mia from kindergarten and homeschooled her because her kindergarten teacher called me in for a conference to let me know that Mia was way too advanced for kindergarten and she did not think it was beneficial to keep her there. The principal, however, would not allow the move to first grade because of her age, so I did what was best for Mia. It was the best decision I could have ever made. As a result, I had to change my shift at work to 5:00 p.m. until 1:00 a.m. Dan got his wish in a way because I was home all day. We both were happy with this new schedule. On my way to work, I dropped the children off for swimming lessons, and Dan picked them up on his way home from work. Eventually, we agreed to homeschool Kyle also. I was no longer there for dinnertime but Dan was. That was just the sacrifice we had to make for our children and we were both in agreement.

This arrangement worked for four years until I developed adult onset asthma. I worked at a car rental company and for-tunately—or unfortunately, depending on who is looking at it—one of my triggers was the fumes from the cars on the job. I was forced to quit my job. Less than one month later, I was offered a job with an airline. Dan was opposed to this as he did not want me working again. I have always loved traveling, and since we had four children and limited disposable income, I thought it would be a great opportunity for the family to have. Dan dis-agreed; he had some valid points. Working with the airlines involved working possibly different shifts every time there was a shift bid. Some of the shifts began as early as 4:30 a.m., and the last shift was scheduled to end at 11:00 p.m. but could really end later, especially in the wintertime.

After a lot of discussion between Dan and I, we still could not agree. By this time our children's ages were twenty-one, nineteen, fourteen, and eight. We decided to have a family discussion. I really wanted to accept the job and Dan really did not want me to take it. It was just part-time, so I could not understand his opposition. Together with the kids, we discussed the pros and cons of taking a part-time job with the airlines. We all discussed the fact that every child would have more responsibility as I would be working on weekends and not available for some of my regular weekend chores. I think all that my children got out of the discussion was the fact that they could have an opportunity to travel and see different parts of the world that they otherwise would not be able to see.

At the end of the discussion, it was agreed by all, including Dan, that I would take the job. I worked with that airline for ten years and Dan never took advantage of the benefits, not even one time. I sometimes wondered if that was him being passive-aggressive about not getting his way. However, thanks to the airlines my children and I have collectively visited Grenada, Trinidad and Tobago, Barbados, Jamaica, Hawaii, Canada, France, Spain, Scotland, Wales, Switzerland, Ireland, England, Italy, the Bahamas, Mexico, Beijing, St. Martin, Ghana, Martinique, Aruba, Anguilla, St. Thomas, Puerto Rico, and St. Vincent. That is just internationally. We traveled domestically to too many places to mention.

Nick, being twenty-one when I started working with the airlines, did not have an opportunity to travel with us as he had an independent life living on his own. The two younger children did the most traveling. Simone went to Paris to study the summer before her senior year of college. Dan promised he was going to accompany us when we visited her, but he never did. I paid $63 (USD) for three first-class round-trip tickets to Paris. At $21 a person, Dan still refused to go, much to the annoyance of my friends and family, who could not understand my degree of tolerance. What no one knew was that Dan was petrified of flying. I traveled with Dan a couple of times to Trinidad and once to Martinique and the experience was horrendous. I really believed in my heart that if I insisted on Dan traveling with us each time, that I could cause him to have a heart attack from the experience and I did not want that responsibility.

Whenever Dan did travel, he had to take either a valium or an alcoholic drink. For days prior to a trip he would be in a different mood. When he worked in Atlanta, he only had to travel once a year, usually to his job's head office in Utah. He never got used to the trip. Every year he would try to talk himself into why he should not go, but he went anyway. The kids and I always felt sorry for him, though they still begged him to come with us on trips at different times. In the end, we all accepted that his extreme fear and anxiety of flying could be detrimental to his wellbeing. It was not a responsibility we cared to have.

We went to Jamaica many times, only paying $9 a person round-trip, and again we traveled first class. That was a two-hour flight out of Atlanta, and Dan had a close friend who lived in Jamaica that he never visited. As a family, the only time we all ever traveled together was on the way back from my dad's funeral, six months after I started to work with the airlines.

Dan, the Family Man

Dear Mistress Ali,

Let me tell you about my husband. Dan was caring, thoughtful, and romantic. With Dan, my children and I felt safe and protected. We had what one would call an old-fashioned marriage. In our marriage, our roles were very defined and accepted by both of us. In today's world, all the liberated women in society—maybe you included—would not understand. However, it is what worked for us. My role was to take care of the home, my husband, and my children. Dan's role was that of provider, protector, and leader. Along the way, due to circumstances beyond our control, the roles were sometimes reversed, which we both accepted without hesitation.

Dan was not what one would call a modern-day dad who was friends with his children. Dan was the kind of dad that I grew up with. My mom was a stay-at-home mom and my dad was the bread-winner and disciplinarian. They raised seven children with morals and values, with family being a priority. My parents were married for fifty-seven years when my dad passed away.

Family was important to Dan. He was loved by his nieces and nephews, and my nieces and nephews. He had close relationships with his sisters. He was not as close with his two brothers, but he loved them and they loved him. When Mia was baptized on Thanksgiving weekend in 1990, my entire family, which consisted of twenty-nine people at the time, drove up from Florida and everyone stayed at our home. That weekend, which consisted of four days, will be remembered as one of the most fun, memorable weekends of our life. Dan cooked and entertained for the entire weekend. I had the young baby at the time, so I was of little help to him. Dan had no complaints about all that work. As a matter of fact, as a result of that weekend, we made it a new family tradition for everyone to come to Atlanta for Thanksgiving. In addition to our immediate family, Dan and I extended invitations to anyone who had nowhere to go for Thanksgiving. To this day, twenty-four years later, the tradition continues. Of course the family has more than tripled in size, so the younger generation may spend the holiday weekend with their respective families. My siblings and their spouses, together with some of their children, continue to come.

Sunday at our home was always a day spent with family and our friends who visited, either invited or uninvited, it never mattered to us. If we had friends who lived alone, they were always invited to our home for dinner on a Sunday. When my nephew attended Morehouse College, he was always welcomed at our home with any of his friends who had a desire to have a home-cooked meal, whether it was just for the weekend or a holiday. Dan and I were always in agreement, helping anyone any time we needed to. When our older children attended college, their friends were also always welcomed.

When a friend of Dan's was experiencing problems during her divorce, Dan and I kept her children almost every weekend as she had to work two jobs to survive and we did not want the children to be alone on the weekend. I sometimes worked on the weekend, especially on some Saturdays. That made no difference to Dan. He let the children come over and everyone was fed and supervised and taken care of.

We had another friend who had problems with her husband. Who did she turn to for help and advice? No other than Dan. There were several occasions when my friend and her husband came over to talk to Dan as he was respected and kind and always seemed to make an impact in a positive way.

We also had two friends who were single parents of two teenage boys who were beginning to exhibit some discipline issues in school and at home. The mothers felt frustrated and alone. They turned to Dan, who in turn would go to the respective homes and have a talk with the young men. Again, there was always a positive outcome and the mothers could not stop thanking Dan for his help, advice, and support.

Neither Dan nor our four children liked store-bought bread. As far back as I could remember, the first year in our marriage, Dan began to bake bread every Saturday night. This became a tradition that was developed and continued for as many years as we were married. Every Saturday night, when the kids were growing up, we would watch television while Dan made the bread. The children would be tired and sleepy, but it was literally impossible to get any of them to go to bed until that bread came out of the oven. No matter how they were falling asleep on themselves, once I suggested that they go to bed they became wide awake until that bread came out of the oven and they had a couple of slices of hot bread with butter. Sometimes they would have the bread with cheese, but usually everyone just wanted bread and butter. After we had devoured a couple of loaves, then and only then would any of the children willingly go to bed.

Dan was also wonderful to my parents. When my dad was getting on in age, he began to be less inclined to accept invitations from his friends to visit them at their homes. My mom, on the other hand, was always ready to accept the invitations. This caused a little conflict between them sometimes. On one occasion when we visited my parents, they were having a discussion and my mom was upset. Upon inquiring about the situation, it was explained to Dan and I that my parents were invited to a friend's house for dinner. My parents got dressed, but when my uncle arrived to transport my parents my dad decided that he did not want to go anymore. My uncle left and my parents were left at home, much to my mom's annoyance. Dan listened to the story, then tried to coax and encourage my dad to change his mind. Dan told me to go and open the car door, and before anyone could blink, he picked my dad up in his arms as if he were a six-month-old baby and put him in the car. All the while, my dad kept saying, "Put me down, put me down." Dan joked, "Dad, I gave you an opportunity to do it the easy way or the hard way. You chose the hard way." My mom got into the car and Dan drove them to the friend's house. My mom could not stop laughing. Even my dad had to laugh. After that day, any time my dad was being stubborn for no reason, my mom would say, "Do you want me to call Dan?" That usually took care of the issue. My parents loved Dan like a son instead of a son-in-law and he would have done anything for them.

One day while I was at work, one of my coworkers came and told me about one of her friends from another airline who was recently diagnosed with cancer. She also told me that the young lady with cancer was having a very difficult time financially. She mentioned this to a few of us, so we made a decision to try and help the young lady. After some discussion, we decided to have a fundraiser selling hotdogs or something. I immediately volunteered my husband to help cook the food. I could make that offer without even discussing it with Dan beforehand because that was the kind of man he was. When I did come home and asked him if he would help, the only thing he wanted to know was how many lunches we were trying to sell. I told him as many as he wanted. Dan cooked food, set it up in the serving pans, packed it in my vehicle for me to transport to the airport, and told me what to do when we were ready to serve. Together with the other coworkers who cooked, we made over $1,300 on that day and the young lady with the cancer diagnosis was forever grateful.

Together with contributions from other coworkers and Dan, we repeated this on another occasion when one of our coworker's mother passed away suddenly. The mother's body had to be sent to another state for burial. This coworker was one of the youngest employees in our company, so everyone got involved to help with the cost of the funeral and service.

As I mentioned earlier, Dan was a real family man and dad. Every Christmas, as long as we had been a family, we drove to Florida. Even though I had airline benefits for the last ten years of our life together, as I also mentioned earlier, Dan was petrified of flying. We usually left on the last day that Dan worked before Christmas. Dan would come home from work and go directly to bed. While he slept, the children and I would clean the house, do all the laundry, pack for the trip by making sandwiches, and then the boys would pack the car. When we were all ready, we would wake Dan. We would get into the car with our pillows and blankets and we would leave for Florida around midnight. Dan preferred this time as he liked to drive when everyone else was sleeping and he could drive in peace and quiet with just his music for company. We did this every year while we were married and we continued the tradition to this day, except now we leave in the day instead of the night.

When I worked with the airline in Atlanta, I usually worked the early morning shift, which started at 4:30 a.m. I did this for ten years and I left home at 3:45 every day. There was not one day in the ten years that I did this shift that Dan did not interrupt his sleep at 3:45 a.m. every morning to stand at the door and tell me goodbye and see me get into my car and drive off. In the beginning I felt bad seeing him get out of his bed and interrupt his sleep. Dan assured me, however, that he could go right back to sleep, so it did not matter. He hated that I had that shift but recognized that it worked better for the children as I was home by 1:30 p.m. I was home in time to take a nap, prepare dinner, and pick the kids up from school. This was Dan, the good guy and loving father, son, and son-in-law.

When we were married for twenty-five years, Dan decided to have a huge anniversary party. At first I was reluctant about having the party as I felt it was going to be too much of a financial strain, but Dan insisted and since he was the one who managed our finances, being an accountant by profession, it was not long before I was on board with the party idea. Dan had begun making plans with our oldest daughter and I had limited input except for finding the venue. Our family and friends came from Trinidad, Canada, New York, Pennsylvania, and Florida to attend the event. It was a great party, and in the end I was truly happy that Dan had insisted. During the planning stage, Dan, in an effort to surprise me, found and purchased the tune we danced to at our wedding, "Make it with You," sung by a group called Bread. Some of the words to the tune are as follows:

Life can be short or long
Love can be right or wrong
And if I chose the one I'd like to help me through
I'd like to make it with you
I really think that we could make it, girl

I had not heard that tune in several years. In 2000, things were not as accessible as they are today on YouTube and the Internet. Imagine my complete surprise when during Dan's speech at the party he began to tell our guests about the song we danced to at our wedding and he broke into song. Pretending to have difficulty singing, he turned to the DJ and said, "DJ, help me out," and then the DJ began to play our tune. I was truly overcome with emotion when I got up to dance to our tune that we had danced to twenty-five years ago. I will never forget the feeling I had at that moment as I considered that to have been the most romantic thing that Dan had done for me, and he was a romantic guy. That moment made the party, the expenses, and the work in preparation all worth it.

Some friends and family contributed to the magic of that night with speeches in which they all congratulated Dan and me on our twenty-fifth-year milestone. Everyone expressed love and support; some were serious, some were humorous, but they were all appreciated. My younger brother ended his speech with the line, "Once again, I would like to congratulate Dan and Eva for reaching this milestone and raising four wonderful children. I wish them another twenty-five happy years; however, if Eva and Dan should ever end in divorce, we want Dan."

Never in a million years could I or anyone at that party have imagined that six years following that magical, romantic night I would be in a position where I would be fighting to save my crumbling marriage, six years after Dan stood before all our close friends and family members and publicly professed his love to his wife and children. Dan described me as the peak in the marriage and he described himself as the valley. Dan described me as having a great personality and being a good-times person, while he considered himself to be more reserved and the person responsible for holding everything together. When he spoke about the children, he said, "Over the years, we have raised four children and that has been a challenge; however, I would not trade anyone in my family for the world. Even though my wife and children find me to be a little picky, when I look at my kids I am proud of who they are. I am not going to change for the simple reason that it works. I love my wife and my kids 'til death do us part."

Discovering the Mistress

May 2006

Dear Mistress Ali,

My husband Dan, to whom I was married at the time for thirty years, came to me and told me he was going to be out of town on Memorial weekend as he was attending a men's retreat. I did not believe him at the time because the Friday before that weekend I was scheduled for a simple surgical procedure. Though simple, I would have required the assistance of my husband. Instead of being there for me he made the retreat his priority, and I thought that was very odd for three reasons. One, Dan did not really belong to any church group, service organization, or any other group for that matter. Two, he could not give me the name of any one of the men who were supposed to be accompanying him on this trip. He kept promising me the list of names but never did give me anything. The third reason for my dubious position was the fact that Dan, my husband of thirty years, would have never let me have that surgical procedure without being there for me. He was not that kind of husband.

July 2006

My youngest daughter was participating in a pageant on a Sunday afternoon. Dan did not want to go. I did not think anything of it at the time and decided to take her; my oldest daughter decided to accompany me. Just as we were ready to leave the house, Dan said, "Since you all are going to be gone for the day, I think I am going to find somewhere to go myself." Again, this was totally out of character. Dan was a family man and Sundays were usually spent with our kids. Dan had few friends and all of his friends' wives were my friends, whom he would never have visited on a Sunday without his own family. My two daughters and I attended the pageant preliminaries and then went out to dinner. Upon returning home at approximately 9:00 p.m., I discovered Dan was not at home. This was very surprising because earlier that day Dan, our youngest daughter, and I attended church and then visited our oldest daughter. While at her house, he assisted her and her husband with some home repairs. We got back home and I left two hours later with the girls for the pageant. Returning home at 9:00 p.m. indicated a very long and tiring day for me, but more so for Dan, who had performed actual physical labor at our daughter's house. For him not to have been at the house when I returned was highly unusual and very suspicious. At 9:30 p.m. I called him and he was quick to respond with, "I will be home shortly." At that time

I worked at a job that required me to be at work at 4:30 a.m., so I was usually in bed by 11:00 p.m. At 10:30 that night, as I got ready for bed, Dan was still not home. I went to bed, but because I was suspicious I locked my bedroom door. Dan would have to interrupt my sleep in order to gain access into the room. He came in at 1:00 that Monday morning.

My suspicions were now elevated. That Monday evening, Dan came in from work, had dinner, and fell asleep in front of the TV. I attempted to go and search his car as I was convinced that something was going on. In our thirty years of marriage there had been only one time that I had ever searched my husband's briefcase. However, I had a gut feeling that something was not right with us and Dan was doing too many things that were out of character for him. When he fell asleep, I took his car keys and attempted to get into his car to look around. My adrenaline was running high and I was nervous. I put the key in the door, and as I turned it the car alarm went off. I ran back inside, put the keys on the kitchen table, and ran into the den to give the impression that I was watching TV. Fortunately, the noise of the alarm did not interrupt his sleep. This was, again, very unusual for him.

The next morning, on my day off, he awoke and did not see his keys on the bedside where he left them the night before. He said in a state of panic, "Did you move my car keys?" I said, "Yes, I went in your car to look for my earring that I misplaced after church yesterday. Your keys are on the kitchen table." At this time it was six in the morning. He jumped out of bed, retrieved his keys from the kitchen, and next I heard the chimes for the security system alerting me that he was going outside. He came back inside looking relieved and proceeded to go into the shower to get ready to leave for work at seven. At this point I was convinced that my suspicions must be right since my touching his car keys seemed to have created great anxiety for him. Dan went into the shower and I decided to check his cell phone. To my horror and complete devastation, I heard your message that you apparently left him the night before.

Clearly you were fully aware that he came in on Monday night, had dinner, and decided to take a nap. The message you left on his cell phone was, "Hi, just checking to see if you got up from your nap, bye. Talk to you later, love you." I took the phone with trembling hands and went into the bathroom. I asked him to open the shower door, which he did. I held up his phone and pushed the button to play the message. At first he looked as if he had just seen a ghost, but quickly recovered and went into lying mode. He proceeded to fabricate a story about a student from his job.

I asked, "A student telling you she loves you?"

He grabbed the phone from my hand and told me "No one said 'love you.' You did not hear that."

I lost it at that moment and began to scream at him to tell the truth because I knew what I heard. He proceeded to act like that situation did not take place and continued to get dressed for work. I began to cry to the point of hysteria and he continued to get dressed for work. I could not believe what was happening especially since my husband did not offer any further explanation, did not attempt to even comfort me, just continued to dress and leave for work.

At this point I was completely devastated, broken, hysterical, overwhelmed, and angry. I called Dan on his cell phone and begged him to come back home so we could talk, yet he refused. I begged him to tell the truth. Again, he refused. He continued with his lie. Once Dan got to his office, I continued to call him and try to talk to him. He continued to lie and claim that no one said "love you" on the message. At this point I started to scream and yell and use profane language, which was not something that I did in my normal life. Fortunately and unfortunately, I was unaware that anyone was in my house at the time. I was crying, screaming, and using profanity while trying to get an appropriate response from Dan instead of his lies on top of lies. My son, who heard all this, ran upstairs in a panic because in his twenty-two years on this earth he had never ever heard me use profanity, cry, or behave in that manner. He immediately asked what was wrong.

I replied, "Nothing."

He then implored, "Please tell me what is going on."

I said, "This does not concern you. It is none of your business."

He said, "It is my business because I know what this is about."

I started to apologize because I assumed that he heard what I had been screaming to Dan and figured it out.

He interrupted me and said, "Mom, I know that Dad is having an affair. We all know but did not want to tell you."

I almost collapsed at that point from the knowledge that my children could possibly have known something that I had no clue about until that morning. I then partially composed myself and

29

asked him to tell me what he thinks he knows. He then proceeded to tell me what Mia, his younger sister and our last child, told him. While in the car with her dad on mornings when he takes her to school, he talks on the phone. Mia told Kyle that one morning when she got in the car and put on her headphones, before she turned on her iPod, she heard her dad on the phone and assumed he was talking to me. She said he usually puts his Bluetooth in his ear, his phone in the console, and she puts on her headphones and listens to her music. She told her brother that she heard him say something about "my daughter," which alerted her that he could not have been speaking to me. The next day she put on her headphones but deliberately did not turn on her music. She then listened to Dan's conversation and realized it was no ordinary conversation. According to my son, the next time Dan got on the phone, Mia paid attention and was able to report to him that her dad gets on the phone and talks to someone whose name is Ali. She memorized your name and number from his phone in the console.

Apparently, my son Kyle could not handle this information, so he told our oldest son, Nick, who told our oldest daughter, Simone. At that point, my four children began to monitor their father's pattern of behavior and confided in each other. They all agreed that it was not a good idea to tell me. This was the beginning of the end of my marriage. Throughout that day I continued to beg and plead with Dan to come home so we could talk. He refused until I threatened to go to his job with my two sons. By this time Kyle had apparently called Nick and informed him of what was going on. Dan did not want to see his sons and wife at his job, so he came home.

Dan arrived home with a whole lot of attitude, no remorse, no truths, and a cold heart. I did not know who that person was. Dan did not seem to care about the turmoil he started in our family. He immediately began to blame me for involving our children in our business. Ironically, he had been the one to be so irresponsible, immature, and behaving like a teenager that he could not wait the thirty minutes it took to drop our daughter off at school to talk with his mistress. He had to do it with his fifteen-year-old daughter in the car.

I tried to talk to Dan, but with no success. My boys decided they would try to speak with him as men; he ignored them completely, which just ignited the situation. My sons decided at that point to call your number and you answered and spoke to Kyle briefly. You assumed it was Dan on the other end and told my son that you were at the dentist. At this point, there was no doubt that you existed and all the information that my young daughter gave her siblings was true.

That night, while Dan lay in bed acting as though life was as normal as the day before, I tried everything in my power to get him to communicate and speak truthfully. I decided to dial your number myself in his presence and put you on speaker. You answered the phone but I hung up as soon as you said hello. Dan was unmoved by my actions. I did it two more times while Dan sat on the bed and seemed unperturbed by what was going on around him. At this point, I realized that the person sitting on the bed next to me was someone I did not know at all anymore.

The very next morning, while Dan was getting dressed for work I called you using his phone and you answered. I identified myself to you and told you that it was not a good idea to hang up the phone. You took heed. You promptly told me you were unaware that Dan was married. Even though I did not believe you, I acted as though I did and we had a very civilized conversation. At that point you asked me what I wanted you to do and I said to you, "I need for you to call my husband one more time, let him know we spoke, and end your affair with him so I can fix my marriage."

It was my intention at the time to pack all Dan's stuff so he would realize that he could not disrespect and mistreat me. Well, I did not anticipate at the time that when I did that, and he was out of our home, you would have been so eager to welcome him into yours. It was my naive thinking that made me assume that you would keep your word about ending the affair. That way, when I packed his stuff he would realize that he could no longer play the cheating game. He would be forced to have a reality check and know that I would not put up with his cheating and you would not put up with his lies. Well, little did I know that I played right into your hands. You seized the opportunity to invite Dan to move into your home with you.

Dan was extremely angry when I called him at work and told him to come to the house and collect his belongings in the garage. I had an asthma attack that day, went to the doctor, and then went and purchased some new locks for the doors at the house. I changed the locks, changed the security code on the system, then called Dan and told him what I had done.

Dan came home that evening and broke the door from the garage leading to the house. He took his computer, and with the help of the DeKalb county police, moved out all his things. The police came to the house because when he broke the door the alarm was triggered. Since I changed the code, he had no way to turn it off. I removed myself from home after I called him at work because I did not want to be present when he came to the house.

When I returned to the house that night with my oldest son, Nick, Dan was still in the garage, packing his stuff into his vehicle. No words were spoken by any one of us and I had this overwhelmingly sad and painful dose of reality that the person packing the vehicle in the garage was a complete stranger. The reason that I had such a reaction at that moment was in part due to the fact that our son was also present and Dan had not said one word to any of our children since the discovery was made the day before. Dan looked at my son and me with such anger and hate in his eyes that I was left with one question in my mind, "Who is this guy?"

The guy in the garage was not the guy I had been with, at that time, for thirty-one years. That was not the guy I listened to over the decades talk about his absent and negligent father and his devoted mother. That was not the guy who vowed to never hurt his wife and children the way his own father had hurt his mom and his siblings. I never knew his dad as he passed away when Dan was a teenager, but according to him he refused to attend his father's funeral until his older sister convinced him to attend. That was not the guy who some of our friends turned to for advice when they were experiencing problems in their marriage. That was not the guy who lay in bed with me talking about the evils of cheating on your wife and the potential destruction that cheating can cause on a family, and most importantly, on the children. That was not the guy who just a year prior was beaming with pride and joy to walk his oldest daughter down the aisle on her wedding day. That was not the guy who the year before had replaced the diamond in my ring with a bigger one to celebrate our anniversary. He said when we got married thirty years ago that diamond was all he could have afforded, but with our daughter's pending nuptials two weeks before our anniversary he thought it would be nice to do something for me to symbolize our marriage commitment on the same day as our daughter's wedding. I was given the ring with the new and upgraded diamond in the limousine on the way to our daughter's wedding; that was an incredibly special and very memorable day. That was not the guy I dated for three years and then married well over thirty years ago. I had no clue who that stranger was in my garage in the body of my husband.

Moving Out

Dear Mistress Ali,

Since no words were spoken the night Dan left the marital home we shared for sixteen years, neither I nor my children had any idea where he was moving to. We were sure of one thing; it was not to my son or oldest daughter's house. Two days later, Dan returned to our home after work. He came and brought some money for our youngest daughter, Mia. He also bought groceries. The day after that he returned to our home again and cut the grass. I asked Dan then where he had moved to, and he told me he was living at one of his coworkers' home on Larchlemont Drive, in downtown Atlanta. I found it odd because Dan had worked at that job for fifteen years and had a couple of acquaintances but no friends, especially one that he could turn to in a crisis.

35

During this period, Dan remained in contact with friends and family, but unfortunately continued to lie about and deny his affair. I was not yet ready to communicate in a civilized manner with Dan. My hurt, anger, pain, and devastation were still too overwhelming. Every time I had reason to communicate with him, I found my behavior to resemble that of a person I did not know. I was bitter, angry, and felt desperate. I do not quite know if at that time I was thinking clearly. I fought Dan with my words and my profane language. I almost took pleasure in my behavior as Dan was not used to this behavior and did not like it one bit. I did not care and somehow it made me feel powerful, although in reality I had no control over the situation. I had no authority to determine the direction my marriage would take. I was losing my ability to manage my pain and the deep, deep rage I felt toward Dan. During this period, I was not working due to my health. My blood pressure was continuously elevated to dangerous levels. My asthma attacks seemed to be more frequent. My tears, however, seemed to be infinite.

Around my children, I tried to create a facade that I was tough and strong and coping with the situation without shedding a tear. I felt then that tears would make me appear weak, but fighting words and profane language would make me appear tough. That was very far from the truth. I found myself in a situation that I could barely handle and had no idea how it was going to end. I have no regrets about not crying, breaking down, and falling apart in front of the children, especially my fifteen-year-old daughter. I don't think with all that was going on with their dad that they would have been able to cope with a broken mom as well. I do, however, have regrets about the way I behaved because that was not the mother that they knew. My children had never heard me use profanity in their entire life because that was not something that I did. Hearing me behave in that manner every time I had cause to speak to Dan, in hindsight, could not have been good for them. Unfortunately, there are no books or guides on how to behave when put in a situation you never ever thought was a possibility in your happy life with the love of your life.

While Dan continued to live elsewhere, he continued to come to our home every day after work. To this day, I do not know why because I rarely spoke to him. I would, most days, remain locked in my room while he was there. My daughter and son who lived in the home spoke to him briefly and he just hung around. Because of this, I began to believe that he was really living with the aforementioned coworker in Atlanta and felt so out of place that he would come back home to pass the time. One Sunday morning, I called Dan and there were a lot of women talking in the background. One of the voices sounded like yours. I was not sure, and again it made me suspicious about where he was really living. I sent you the following e-mail even though I had no proof he was at your home. It was so early on a Sunday morning I couldn't think of anywhere else he could be.

Eva-Marie

From:
Sent: Thursday, August 24, 2006 12:15 PM
To:
CC:
Subject: Choose 1 for a happy life

Dear Ms.   ,

I will like to inform you that since you knowingly
established an ongoing relationship with my husband
causing undue pain and suffering to my children
especially my fifteen year old, I will be taking the
necessary action that we spoke about on the phone.

The first time I spoke to you on the phone I was really
nice to you in spite of the fact that you were sleeping
with my husband. I believed you when you said you did
not know he was married (which I have on tape). At the
end of our conversation you asked me what I wanted you
to do, I told you "call my husband one more time, let
him know we spoke and then leave him alone."
Unfortunately, it is evident that you lack the ability
to make decisions that are good for you. You continued
to call him (I access his voicemail everyday and
forwarded your messages to my cell phone).

Based on the fact that you are desperate, empty and
needy you made a choice to invite my husband to move in
with you when I put him out. Definitely a poor decision
on your part, at that point it became clear to me that
you obviously have a bruised empty and wounded ego.
Instead of backing off and letting me husband sort his
marriage out, you saw that as an opportunity to seek
your own interest again at the expense of my children.
It is unfortunate that you are so immoral and
desperate. I wonder how your supervisors will feel when
they find out that in your professional life you are
sleeping with an employee whom they consider to be your
subordinate. In your personal life even though you own
your own home and car as you have told me on two of the
three occasions that I spoke to you, in reality you are
nothing but a slut who owns a home and a car.

I gave you fair warning that someone will pay for
hurting my children. I have no intentions of doing
anything illegal or anything to cause you any physical
harm, I leave that behavior to people who break the

law, so please know you have nothing to fear. I only
came to the cul-de-sac to get physical proof of my
husband's presence at your home. You have probably
figured by now that I had access to my husband's e-mail
(unknown to him) I have the tape of our conversation, I
have every voicemail you left my husband. (I had been
checking his voicemail and forwarding the messages you
left him to my cell phone) and last but by no means
least the phone records from 770-235-0000 and 404-245-
0000. I am sure your bosses will love to read and
listen to my evidence, especially since it was the
property of _____ that you guys were using.

I now leave you with two choices (1) _____LEAVE MY
HUSBAND ALONE and I will give you my word not to
involve your bosses or (2) _____ Continue your
affair and allow him to remain in your house and this
will definitely become ugly. I hope for your sake you
make the right choice. Neither my children or myself
have anything more to lose.

Please do not respond to this e-mail with another
email. I have no desire to communicate with you ever
again. Just make a check mark next to your choice and
return this e-mail. Please note that there is not a
third choice to ignore this e-mail as the result will
be the same as the second choice.

A word of advice, work on your self-respect, your
integrity, your morality and try a visit to an adult
store where they sell sex toys and leave married men
alone. Have a good life. God Bless You. You Will Need
It.

Dan's actions seemed so strange that I made a decision to
follow him in my car the next time he left our home. It never
worked out because he would always leave our home when it
was already dark outside and it was very difficult for me to
follow a car at night because of all the car headlights and traffic
lights. However, before Dan had removed his computer from the
home, I found out how to bypass his password and access infor-

mation on his computer. One of the things I was able to access was his contact list. This was where I discovered what your legal name was. After a couple of failed attempts at following Dan to find out where he was really living, I Googled your name and got an address for you. My hunch was that Dan was really living at your house, but he continued to lie and I had no proof. I was forced to accept what he was telling me.

From the time that Dan was no longer in my home until he moved back, my children and I were subjected to prank calls at all hours of the night and especially early morning. I made reports to our telephone carrier and the police, but they were unable to help me. I was sure it was you or someone related to you who was harassing my family, but again I had no proof.

One night when Dan left my house I called my eldest son, Nick, to come to my home to stay with my young daughter. I armed myself with your address and directions and set out to prove that Dan was living at your house. While I was on the way, I called Dan and asked him where he was.

He answered, "I am at the home where I am staying."

I inquired, "Are you at Larchlemont Drive?"

He replied, "Yes, where else would I be?"

I said, "I don't know. I just don't believe that is where you are living."

His following retort was, "Believe whatever the hell you want to believe, that is where I am and I am not going to answer the question again," and hung up the phone.

I continued driving; with every part of my body shaking and my heart pounding, I continued on my mission. The directions brought me to a cul-de-sac. Lo and behold, there was Dan's car. I was close to hysteria at this point. My breathing became difficult and irregular, the beginning signs of an asthma attack. I parked my car directly behind Dan's and I called him on his phone again.

"Were you asleep?"

"I would have been if you were not calling my phone every ten minutes." He answered in a very irritated tone.

Confident now, I asked, "So I suppose you are at Larchlemont?"

He screamed, "For the last time YES! YES! YES!"

Finally, I screamed, with my body almost convulsing, my breathing hard and labored, and my hands and voice shaking, "You are such a f——ing liar! Look out your window. Do you see the lights shining on your car? That is me, you f——ing lying bastard."

I turned my car and started to drive off, but he said, "I am coming outside, hold on."

I said, "Fuck you," and drove off. I then called my sister. In the midst of my bawling, I was also having an asthma attack all alone in my car. My sister tried to help me and suggested that I go straight to the emergency room. I pulled my car on the shoulder of the road to use my inhaler and to try to compose myself, but was terrified that I was going to die at the side of the road in my car. My sister put me on hold for a minute then came back on the phone to find out my exact location because Dan was in the car on the road trying to find me. I told her to tell him to go to hell and where I am is none of his business.

As I continued driving I could only pray to God to let me make it to the emergency room because no one knew my whereabouts and my sister was all the way in Florida. By His grace I started to feel a little better, but I began to pray out loud. Thinking about my children, I prayed to God again to help me make it to the emergency room, which I finally did. By this time I was much calmer and breathing a little better, thanks to my sister, who remained on the phone with me the entire time until she knew I was doing better and safely at the county medical center. I got home around 12:30 a.m. As soon as I got in the house, my second son, who was now home, asked me where I had gone. I told him I had an errand to run. As I was about to go and get ready for bed, at around 12:45 a.m. my phone rang. Kyle and I picked up at the same time, and before I could speak, my son said, "Hello."

The person at the other end was a female and she screamed, "Can I speak to your mother?"

My son, startled at the person's tone and anger, said, "May I ask who is calling?"

At that point the person said, "My fucking name is Ray-Ray, I am Ali's sister. Tell your fucking mother do not ever find her fucking ass on this street again. Tell her to fuck herself and leave my fucking sister alone." She continued to use the most horrible, profane language at my son and continued to behave in a manner that would suggest to anyone listening that I was the mistress and her sister was the wife.

My son hung up the phone and I had to tell him the truth about what had transpired earlier that night. I then instructed my son to call his dad and let him know what just happened. All Dan said to my son was, "Okay." There was no kind of sympathy, shame, sadness, or rage for what was just done to his child or his wife, the mother of his four children.

The next morning I called Dan's sister and told her what took place the night before. When I told her about the sister calling and cursing and threatening my children and myself, my sister-in-law suggested that I make a police report because it appeared to be a dangerous situation for my children and me. I thought that was a good idea, so I called Dan at work and asked him for the name of the person who cursed and threatened his son and me the night before. He asked me why I needed to know and I told him that his sister suggested that I file a police report.

To my surprise and disbelief, Dan answered, "I do not know."

I was in disbelief, "You are living in a house with someone and you do not know their name?"

Well, Dan was unbending and held on to his lie that he did not know her name. Without a last name I was unable to file a police report. That same day my son asked me what his dad was going to do about that woman who called and threatened us. I just said, "Ask your dad."

What was interesting to my sister and Dan's sister was the fact that the woman identified herself to my son as your sister. So the question became why she was so involved and angry. And furthermore, why was she so abusive to my children and me

43

when we had not done anything to any of you and she was not the mistress?

The next day I received this e-mail from your sister:

From:
To:
CC:
Subject: Official Cease and Desist Request (LEAVE MY SISTER ALONE)
Date: Wed, 13 Sep 2006 09:32-0400

Mrs. _____,

I am compelled to notify you in writing that your childish, irratic, and terroristic behavior towards my sister is negatively impacting on my right to the quiet enjoyment of my home. I have resided with my sister in complete comfort and contentment until your recent and escalating campaign of harassment began when you started calling her home, cell, and work phone several weeks ago.

Now that you have added drive-by menacing to your repatoire I must insist that you direct all of your negative energy toward your wayward husband.

It is neither my nor my sister's fault that _____ elected to lie about his marital status. He told her in my presence that he had been divorced for several years. Later he said he had been separated from you for five years and that you did not live in the family home. Later still he changed his story and said you were moving back into the house.

I really don't care what scenario is true. It is more than obvious that _____ does not want you any longer. He has gone to great lengths to ingratiate himself with my sister and insinuate himself in her life.

SHE DID NOT PURSUE HIM!!!!!!!!!! Now that they have decided to embark on a life together the past is moot.

This matter concerns me because you are bringing your petty and pathetic squabble to my residence where I PAY TO LIVE. You and your disrespectful children need to find something constructive with which to occupy your time and stop hurling slurs against my sister's good name.

I have consulted with an attorney _____, ESQ, and he has assured me that I may obtain a restraining order against you for the menacing email you sent my sister and the recent STALKING of our home.

When I leave for work this evening I am going straight to the Lilburn Police Dept. and filing a report about your recent activities. I am also going to the Court House and applying for a restraining order with the Commissioner.

It is illegal in this country to threaten people via the internet. Your persistant calling, emailing, and driving to our home (and calling from outside) is a violation of Stalking laws in the State of Georgia.

I will provide the authorities with your addresses, that of your elder daughter, elder son, and your place of employment so that they may serve you with this restraining order. I will also pursue the assignment of criminal charges against you if this behavior continues.

I have a daughter who is presently away at college. She comes home several weekends during each semester and I will NOT allow you to turn her home into a hostile environment.

You may or may not care about the emotional rollercoaster that you are forcing your children to ride. You will not drag my child along with you.

In your e-mail you boldly stated that you have nothing else to lose..........DON'T FORGET ABOUT YOUR FREEDOM.

Sincerely,

Inbox

Apparently, in addition to being immoral you appear to be a coward. At no point in any of the very civilized conversations I had with you did you express any anger or arrogance, but you decided to keep your sister informed of everything, knowing very well that she was bipolar (according to Dan) and subject to very unpredictable, erratic behavior. I saw that as very passive-aggressive behavior on your part. Two weeks after I sent you that e-mail, your sister decided to contact me, I have to assume with your guidance and instruction. You were copied in the e-mail, so you were fully aware of what was going on and I suppose that it was okay with you, while you sat in the background, to let your sister terrorize my family for no reason other than being Dan's wife and children.

I find the letter so amusing, as should anyone reading it. I never cursed you, threatened you, called you on your home phone, visited you at your home or job (and I knew where you worked). You were sleeping with my husband, your family called my home, threatened and abused my child and myself, your sister called my job several times, your sister called me at all hours in the morning and kept hanging up. You allowed all this to take place and then your sister had the unmitigated gall to say that I was childish and erratic.

At the time that this was going on I found nothing about any of it amusing, not the phone calls, e-mails, or threats. I was in fact very intimidated and fearful of you and your sister. I realized that I was dealing with unstable people who were attacking me simply because I was married to an unfaithful man and I had morals. I had a job where I was highly respected and never shared information about my personal life. I had panic attacks every time I saw a police officer while I was at work. My whole body would begin shaking and I would feel ill. What did I do to any of you? Nothing.

Back Home to Fix The Marriage

Dear Mistress Ali,

Three weeks after the incident Dan called me and asked me to meet him for lunch because he wanted to speak to me about something pertaining to the children and myself. I agreed. After we were finished eating, Dan, without an apology, began to tell me that he would like to come back home and fix our relationship. He explained he wanted his family back and gave reasons, such as being very unhappy living away from his family and that he wanted the situation to end. I listened and asked him why should I allow him to return home. I told him that I did not trust him anymore. He had lied about everything from the beginning, had never admitted anything about the affair, and deep down I did not believe our marriage could be saved.

47

Dan began to tell me how he would do anything in his power to save his marriage, including going to therapy to help him understand why he did what he did. He said he would find the therapist, he would go, and he would be truthful to me in the future. I then asked Dan what I had done or not done that caused him to cheat on me. He then told me that it had nothing to do with me; it was his issue. Dan then lost his mind—after I agreed to allow him to move back home and fix our fractured marriage—by informing me that after he moved back home he would have to return to your house for a couple of Saturdays, claiming that the night your sister called and cursed at and threatened my children and myself that he was so very angry that he did damage to your house. I slipped back into profanity mode and told Dan to f—— off and do not contact me again until he was serious.

He brought up that he'd been threatened that if he did not repair the damage he had created the police would be called and he would be in serious trouble. I insisted that he needed to call his friend Wayne, who did home repairs, and have him go and repair the damage. He insisted that he did not want Wayne in his business. I asserted that when he is serious about coming back home he can give me a call and hopefully I would still be willing to work on our marriage, but it was unacceptable and crazy for him to think that I would willingly participate in having his arranged visits with his mistress. I got up to leave the restaurant.

Dan grabbed my hand and conceded, "Okay, I will work something else out about the repairs. I really would like to move back home on Saturday and start the healing process."

I reluctantly agreed. In my heart I was not sure if that was the right decision. Dan caused my children and me such pain and heartache and showed no real signs of remorse. On the other hand, I thought about how we'd been together for so many years and had raised four wonderful children who were very happy and proud of their parents for having a marriage as long as we had. I felt very conflicted about what the right decision was, but since Dan did so much talking and pleading about wanting his life back with his wife and children, I decided after speaking to my sister and his sister that I needed to give him a chance. The sad truth is that if Dan never picked up the phone and called me to meet with him and asked me to let him move back home I never ever would have done that, so our marriage would have ended at that point. I had my pride, my family, friends, and children, so there was no need to beg Dan for anything other than financial support. Even that was not completely necessary because from the time Dan left the home, until October when he returned, he paid all the bills and bought groceries as he had been in the habit of doing for all the years we were married.

All the weeks that Dan spent out of the house he visited every evening and even acted as if he was still living there. Not one time did I ever call Dan and ask him to come by, and I rarely spoke to him when he was at the house. I never understood what he was telling you or where you thought he was every afternoon after work. You told me at a later date that Dan told you that I had left the marital home and left our fifteen-year-old daughter there alone. You were stupid enough to believe him or you accepted the fact that when you are sleeping with someone else's husband the expectation of ever being told the truth is nonexistent. That was acceptable to you. Just to set the record straight, in case you did not believe me before, I never left the marital home, not then or now. I never put my children in a position to feel abandoned. Dan is a pathological and compulsive liar. I told you that, but you chose to believe his lies because in the end it benefited you to do so.

Dan moved back home in the early part of October, found a therapist, and left work early every Tuesday to attend his session. I was asked to attend the first session with Dan. I was not happy on the first day of meeting the therapist because she was an older, gentle female and I knew beyond a shadow of a doubt that Dan would manipulate her. After hearing about our problem during the very first session, Dr. K made it very clear to Dan that the only way she could help us was if we were prepared to be completely truthful. She also told Dan in order for her to help us he had to sever all communication with his mistress. There were to be no e-mails, no texts, no lunches or dinners, no visits, and absolutely no phone calls. Dan agreed, and expressed that in order to save his marriage he would do anything and everything that was expected of him.

The first question Dr. K asked Dan was if he was happy with his relationship with his wife. Dan answered that he was not and had not been for some time. Dr. K asked him to define "some time." Dan claimed, with me sitting right next to him, that he had been unhappy for the past ten years. I was stunned and speechless by that response. Dr. K then asked me if I was aware of that. I explained to her that six years ago Dan wanted to celebrate our twenty-fifth wedding anniversary with a party with family and friends. I wanted to go on a cruise with him and the children to celebrate in a more intimate way. Dan, however, gave me his argument that he wanted all his close friends and family present to celebrate with him the happiest twenty-five years of his life and I reluctantly agreed. Dr. K asked Dan if what I said was true, and he admitted that it was.

Again Dr. K tried, "When did you become unhappy? Did you become unhappy immediately following the party?"

Still, Dan said no.

By the end of that session I already knew that my marriage was not going to be fixed. Dr. K made it clear in the very beginning that honesty was the first prerequisite to beginning the healing process. From the onset, to almost every other question that was asked Dan did not give a truthful answer. The sad part was that Dr. K did not know the truth from a lie, and that was the only session where I was going to be present to dispute his lies. After that session, Dr. K saw us individually until she decided to see us together again.

Without Dan's knowledge I continued to monitor his phone calls and his messages, and as expected, he was still in communication with you. Your number appeared on his phone almost every day and it was always as incoming calls. You left messages referring to him in the most affectionate terms, calling him "honey" or "babe," and never failing to say "I love you" at the end of your messages, which I always deleted. Somehow Dan believed that if he did not call you and instead you called him it was not considered communicating with you.

Every week that I went to therapy, I got into debates with Dr. K because all she saw in her office was a very remorseful, contrite Dan. I tried to tell her about the phone calls, etc., and her response to me was to stop checking his phone so I wouldn't find the calls. Needless to say I did not agree. I had no intention of trusting Dan as long as he continued to be in contact with you, regardless of who initiated contact. I will never be in a relationship with two people. I respect myself and have too much self-worth to be with someone determined to have a mistress. I have pride and self-respect, and I made myself very clear to Dan on many, many occasions. I would not be in a relationship with him as long as he was in a relationship with that whore.

Dan continued to lie, I continued to investigate, and we both continued to go to therapy. His only argument to me about communicating with you was that he never called you or got in touch with you. He claimed that it was always you calling him and contacting him. Of course I did not believe him. My theory was that he probably called you all day while you all were at work, but he set you up to make it appear to be the truth when he showed me his phone to prove that there was not one time where he called you. I suppose this is what he also told Dr. K and why she believed that you were the problem, not Dan. I knew better because I knew that Dan did not care who he lied about, whether it was you, me, or his children. It did not matter as long as he appeared to be truthful and made himself look good.

In late November of that year, you had a death in your family and there were not any calls on Dan's phone. I do not know if you two were communicating, but I did not think you were because Dan was very different for that couple of weeks. He behaved as if he really wanted his marriage and was working at it for the first time in months. I truly became very hopeful and felt at that time that I had made the right decision about trying to fix my marriage. For the first time in sixteen years, we did not have the entire family over for Thanksgiving as I was not in a good place mentally and emotionally, and my family understood. In December, we went to Florida for Christmas as usual. We would drive down to Florida, visit with Dan's family, and continue traveling to spend Christmas with my family. On the way back we would stop again and visit with Dan's family and sometimes we would stay overnight, then continue on our journey home. That year, during our period of repairing our marriage, everything was a bit better than normal. Dan bought me the most beautiful gift and appropriately written Christmas card. Dan seemed very determined to repair the damage that he had caused in our marriage. The children felt very much at peace because Dan and I presented a very united front to everyone. Just before we left for Florida, Dan suggested that we suspend our therapy until after the holidays and resume in the New Year.

In mid-January we resumed therapy but it seemed to coincide with a change in Dan's attitude. He began to appear withdrawn and disconnected, so once more I began my investigation, only to find a voicemail from you.

Workplace Misconduct

Dear Mistress Ali,

The night before Valentine's Day Dan presented me with a beautiful bouquet of roses, a stuffed animal, and an iPod. That made me very happy, but curious at the same time. I could not understand why he could not have waited until the next day, which was actually Valentine's Day, as he had done our entire life together. The afternoon of Valentine's Day, I called Dan to take him out to dinner but he claimed he had a couple of tax appointments. I got a little annoyed and asked him to change his appointments to the next day. He did, quite reluctantly, and came home in a very foul mood, which ruined the rest of the evening. He then said he did not want to go to dinner because everywhere was going to be crowded and the wait times were going to be too long.

I was not at a place where I would expend any more energy on an issue such as that, so I let it go and we went nowhere that day. However, I had a feeling that I was interrupting a plan that he might have had. I had no proof of this, it was just a feeling. I also had a feeling that you were once again back in our lives.

The following day, Thursday, Dan came home and told me he was going out of town on Saturday to help someone with a job. He could not give me any details, not the last name of the person he would be working with, where he was staying, what the job entailed, or any such answers that he would have ordinarily volunteered. He also told me that he wanted to take me out to dinner on Friday night before he left because he was really sorry about how Valentine's Day turned out. We went to dinner on Friday night and he tried to act normal; I was just not feeling it. On Saturday morning, just before Dan left for his Brunswick trip, I asked him again where he was going to be staying.

His response was, "I do not know. When I get there I will call you." At that very moment his cell phone rang and he answered it. "Hi, what's up? I am leaving in ten minutes." I could not understand what the person was saying, but he was clearly unaware that the volume on his phone was turned up. I heard enough to know that it was a female on the other end of his phone. He continued to talk for a few minutes.

When he hung up the phone, I queried, "Who was that?"

Dan declared, "That was Tony. He was checking to see what time I was leaving."

I snapped, "You are such a lying bastard. That was a woman on the phone. I was hearing her voice."

Without missing a beat Dan offered, "It was Tony's wife." Of course that infuriated me because Dan was turning into such a compulsive liar. I began to accuse him of going away with his mistress and I threatened to follow him when he left. He didn't seem to care. When he got into his car, I got into mine and decided to follow him all the way to see exactly who he was picking up. About five minutes into the drive, I thought to myself that no man was worth this. If he wants to lie and cheat there is nothing I can do, so I turned my car around and went back home.

Even though Dan denied that he was going anywhere with a female I did not believe him. Dan returned on Sunday night. He did not ever give me any information about where he stayed in Brunswick. When he arrived in Brunswick, he called to say he arrived safely and that he hoped that I can believe and trust what he was telling me. He said as soon as they checked into the hotel he would call and give me the information. He never did. When he returned on Sunday, because of my suspicions, I decided that I was going to check his briefcase to see if I could prove that he had been lying all along. I found nothing to indicate who he really spent the weekend with or any hotel information from the weekend trip.

To my surprise, what I found in his briefcase instead was a restaurant receipt from a Valentine's Day lunch. My husband's boss, who was the center's director, had taken you and Dan out to lunch that day using the company's credit card. Because it was the company's credit card, everyone had to sign the back of the receipt. That information broke me and confirmed my original belief that you always knew that Dan was married because I know the center director. She has known me as long as Dan has worked there and she even knew when our last child was born. I attended Christmas parties that the company had. She was not a personal friend of mine, but evidently she was a personal friend of yours. I was devastated because I realized at that time that there were too many forces working against me rather than with me to save my marriage.

I confronted Dan with receipt in hand; he could not deny what was in black and white. I asked him why his boss would do that, and if it had been strictly business, why would he not tell me it happened. He said the reason that Angela, the center director, did that was because you were in a position to do favors for Angela, so that's why she took you to lunch. Because Dan was the director of finance, he was responsible for reconciling the credit card accounts for the center director and that was the reason he had the receipt in his briefcase. Of course, Dan was not forthcoming with that information with either me or Dr. K.

I was so deeply devastated and supposedly desperate to save my marriage, I decided to call Angela and ask to meet with her. I never heard from her. The only way I knew that she ever received my message was because Dan came home that day, quite enraged, and said, "You are going to make me lose my job." He explained that Angela called him into her office and asked what his wife wanted to speak to her about. She discussed that she didn't want to be involved in his personal life as long as he was doing his job. When Dan repeated his boss' words to me, I felt quite deflated and realized I was fighting a losing battle. Apparently, according to Dan, you were senior in the company to Angela and she was his boss, so to them it seemed that I was the problem. Every time after that, when I made a reference to the fact that what was going on with you and Dan was workplace misconduct, Dan would always remind me that if I said anything to anyone I would make him lose his job. So I kept silent.

I feel very angry toward Angela because after I became separated from Dan I found out that he had had an affair with a nonmanagement employee and the employee accused him of sexual harassment. That employee was discharged after Angela's investigation. Yet when her financial director, Dan, was in an extramarital affair with her boss, what did she do? She took them out to lunch on Valentine's Day at the company's expense. This is demonstrative of the double standard allowed for her personal gain. The reason that I was given by Dan to explain the luncheon was that it was a farewell lunch as you had been recently promoted to a new position in the Washington, DC, area.

Visits to Brunswick

Dear Mistress Ali,

The weekend of March 30 to April 2, Dan told me that he had to make a trip to Brunswick and Jacksonville for work, and again I did not believe him, but I could not prove anything. I knew that you had relocated to Washington, so I had no idea about his weekend trip. When Dan left on Friday, I called the bank to check on his recent purchases. I discovered that he had bought gas in Brunswick. I set up a telephone access code, and using his Social Security number, I was able to access all of his bank transactions on a daily basis. He, conversely, was completely unaware of this. On Sunday night, I again called the bank. I found out that he had paid $171 at a Lilburn car rental. When he got home, I asked him if he had rented a car for the weekend. He denied that.

Unbeknownst to him, I told him, "The car rental company called and said that you forgot something in the car and they were putting it in the mail for you."

Dan again denied it. "I don't know what you are talking about. I did not rent any car this weekend."

The next four days we received no mail, not even junk mail. I found this very odd, so I made a trip to the post office to inquire about it. I was told that Dan called and had his mail stopped, but since mail cannot be stopped for one individual in a household, all the mail was stopped and waiting to be picked up. I was livid and enraged. Now I knew beyond any doubt that Dan was lying about everything. I assumed that since your home was in Lilburn, and that is where the car was rented, you had to have been in Georgia for the weekend. I said nothing to Dan that night. When he went to bed, I went into his wallet, got his driver's license number, and got on the Internet. I went to the car rental website, put in his last name and his driver's license number, and there on the computer was a receipt for the most recent car rental for him, March 30 to April 2. I printed it.

The next day I put the receipt on the computer desk where he sat every night to do tax preparation for his clients. I highlighted the dates of the rental, his last name, and the cost of the rental. When Dan came in that night and got on the computer, I watched him pick up the receipt and I proceeded to ask him if he wanted to continue with his lie by claiming that he did not rent a car. He maintained his denial, stating that it was his coworker who rented it. The alleged coworker didn't have a credit or debit card, so he put it in his name as a favor to this coworker. I was enraged and almost out-of-control angry. I called him a liar and demanded that the only way he rented a car for a coworker was if their name was Ali. I continued, "I suppose the whore is in town and you both took a trip to Brunswick and Jacksonville and now you are making up lies as you go along to protect the nasty whore."

Dan put the receipt on the chair, claimed that I was delusional, and proceeded to turn on the computer to begin his clients' taxes. I, on the other hand, could not deal with the person in front of me; he had little to no regard for my pain, anger, or tears that were being caused by his cheating and lying. I asked him why he stopped the mail from coming to the house and informed him at that point that the car rental company never called and left any message about finding anything in his car and therefore there was nothing coming in the mail to him. I discontinued the stop that he put on our mail delivery.

All Dan said to that was, "I stopped my mail from coming to the house; I never stopped yours."

I asked him why, if he had nothing to hide, he stopped his mail delivery, and all he said was, "Because I could."

I felt each time that Dan and I had an argument we were growing farther and farther apart and that I did not know who he was anymore. By this time, we had both discontinued visits to Dr. K. Once I discovered that Dan and you had gone to lunch on Valentine's Day, I decided I was done. I was not the person cheating and lying. Dan was the one begging to save his marriage and yet he was not prepared to be honest about anything, not with me or with the therapist. Clearly Dan was also lying to you, but apparently you were so determined and desperate to be with my husband that you did not care.

Once I told Dan that I was no longer going to therapy he said, "If you are not going to go, I am not going either, because we both need to be going to make this marriage work. I want my family and my marriage and I really want us to continue."

I refused to go. I began to think at that point that Dan was beginning to experience some form of mental illness. He claimed he wanted his marriage and his family. He found a therapist and went every Tuesday, yet he continued to lie to her. He continued to lie to me and was still in a relationship with you. How can anyone explain that?

My birthday was three days after the incident with the receipt and Dan's lies. Dan came home and took me to dinner, bought me a beautiful gift, and while we were having dinner Dan talked to me as if everything that had been going on for the past few months was just a nightmare and not real. Dan was cheerful and talked about plans to open a business in Brunswick. I asked him how that would be possible when I work in Atlanta and he proceeded to explain that I would not have to work anymore once the business was up and running.

For those couple of hours at dinner, I don't know if it was the wine that I drank or if I began to be affected by Dan's mental illness virus, but I actually did not feel the rage or pain I had been feeling in the past. I began to participate in pleasant conversation with Dan and engage in dialogue about future plans, almost as if we were still happily married. I told myself that night I was really going to try and work on my marriage; I was going to make it work. For the first time in my life I felt complete empathy for women who were physically abused. I understood how they were abused and kept going back to their abuser. I had not been physically abused, but I had to be honest with myself and admit that my behavior was the same. Dan was abusing me emotionally and psychologically. He was disrespecting me with his affair and his lies, and I was enraged and emotional. Then three days later he takes me out, wines and dines me, apologizes for what was going on, and then we were back to talking and laughing and making plans for the future. Mentally I knew it was insane, but I felt powerless.

My feelings of euphoria were very short-lived. My birthday was on Thursday, April 5, and on Saturday, April 7, my daughter had to be picked up from a friend's house. Dan left to pick her up. After he left, I saw his open briefcase on the chair with his Palm Pilot in it. I picked it up and started to go through it. I had no means of getting into Dan's e-mail as he had changed the password on his computer. I knew that a Palm Pilot could be linked to a computer since that was a gift from Dan to me on a previous birthday. Once I opened his Palm Pilot and clicked on e-mail, the first one I saw was from you, Mistress Ali. My body and hands started shaking, my heart started racing, and I began to feel like I could not breathe, especially after reading the e-mail. I tried to put the Palm Pilot on the copy machine, but that did not work. I tried to connect the Palm Pilot to the computer and link it to my e-mail, but I was not very computer savvy. Still, I desperately wanted the e-mail. With my mind racing and my heart pounding, I decided to get out a pen and piece of paper and copy the e-mail. I was in the middle of copying it when Dan returned with our daughter and snatched his Palm Pilot from my hand. Your letter, which was dated February 26, and instead of signing your name at the end you signed it "your wife," stated:

"You need not worry about us. No man can come between us. I am committed to you. I have had some fun seeing old friends, but they cannot replace you. I figured I'll do some things before starting my new job. I love you and need you. I have looked into flight info and it will cost $400 to fly into Jacksonville."

That is all I was able to copy. After reading your e-mail, I was able to confirm my suspicions about the previous weekend with the lies about the car rental. You wrote that e-mail soon after you left Georgia in February and you two were making plans to be together that weekend in April. I later learned that you were flying in to visit your daughter in a group home in Jacksonville for her sixteenth birthday, which was on the thirtieth of March. Unfortunately, you didn't see that time alone with your daughter as important. For some reason, you had to visit with your married lover too. Dan did all that he did to deceive me, but he was a sloppy and careless cheater. Everything was discovered with little effort on my part.

The discovery of this letter was another breaking point for me. When I talked to Dan about it, he removed himself from the situation by saying, "That woman is crazy. Have you ever seen anything that I sent to her? When you find something that I sent to her, then you can accuse me. I have no control over what she does."

The next day, which was Easter Sunday, I was still angry and frustrated and fed up with you and Dan. He sat at his computer doing taxes and refusing to have any conversation with me about the situation. I picked up the phone and said to him, "If you are not going to talk, I will call that whore and tell her that she could have you." Dan said nothing.

I dialed your number without blocking mine so you thought that it was Dan and you answered with the most cheerful, exuberant voice. "Happy Easter."

I responded in an angry, deadly tone, "Happy Easter to you too, bitch."

You immediately hung up the phone. I called you again about three times, but you never answered, so I left a couple of messages. Dan sat at the computer doing the taxes, completely unconcerned about what was going on between you and me as I sat next to him. Later that night I received the following e-mail message from you.

Reply | Reply All | Forward | X Delete | Put in Folder ▾ | Print View | Save Address

Subject: RE: Choose 1 for a happy life
From: *You may not know this sender.*
Sent: Sun 4/08/07 4:32 PM
To:

Good Afternoon,

I received your four voice mails and as before I will not disrespect you or your household by calling your home. I just returned from church with my parents and listened to the messages. I had saved this e-mail that you sent me last summer for such an occasion as this. First, my mother answered my phone this morning while I was in the shower and said "that must have been a wrong number, I said 'Happy Easter' and some crazy woman said, 'yea Happy Easter B....' so I hung up." Please make sure you are speaking to me before you go on a rampage, it may not be me on the phone. Let me state the following facts:

1) **I am no longer involved with your husband.**
2) I have moved from Georgia, I still own my home there but left in February of this year. It served as a clean and final break from the "family" drama.
3) I have not corresponded with or spoken to him since just prior to my departure in February.
4) I don't know, nor do I care if he is seeing someone else, for like you I conducted an investigation of my own. However, I will let time and God heal my wounds. I hope that he will also see you through your pain.
5) I have moved on, plan to sell my home in Georgia and purchase another where I reside now.
6) I have met some one new who is most definitely is **SINGLE** like me. I know you do not care about that but I thought I'd let you know that I have moved on. I don't know what he is saying but I have not talked to him so all that remains is between the two of you.
7) If it is that you two can resolve you issues and desire to, I wish you both much success. As for me I really do not wish to engage in any further communication about this or any other subject with you. I have no bad or harsh feelings toward you for you have done nothing to me. I will always remain respectful and courteous. May God bless and keep you through this and any other issues you may face.

Take care

The first line of your e-mail states that *you will not disrespect me or my household by calling my home.* What a joke. You won't disrespect me by calling my home, but you can disrespect me and my children by continuing to sleep with my husband after I begged you to step out of my marriage and allow Dan and I to try and fix things. Your sister used horrible profanity toward my child and myself on my phone in my home, but you want me to make sure I am speaking to you before I say "Happy Easter to you too, bitch"? You considered that a rampage.

In response to your e-mail:

1. That's a lie; you both were together visiting your daughter for her birthday from March 30 to April 2, when Dan rented the car.

2. True, you moved and owned your home, but continued to be the reason for the "family" drama.

3. That is a lie, the e-mail proves it.

4. The nerve of you to conduct an investigation on someone else's husband. His having a wife and four children was not a deterrent? What more could you be investigating? What wounds? Do not bring God into this.

5. I don't care about your house or plans, unless the plan involved leaving my husband alone.

6. Lie, you never broke it off with my husband.

7. My issue was you and you won't remove yourself from my marriage. I think you are as insane as Dan to say you have no harsh feelings toward me. You were sleeping with my husband. You and your family did a lot to my children and me.

One month after finding the e-mail that you wrote Dan, which you signed "Your wife," I discovered something interesting in my husband's car. It was right before a surprise birthday party that was being held for my son's girlfriend. All the invitees were asked to meet at a particular gas station and wait until we got the call to come to the house. While we were waiting in the car at the gas station, Dan left me and went to speak to another parked guest. I have no idea why I began a small, brief search of the car. Maybe it was habit by then or maybe it was just my instinct after all the lies and cheating. Whatever the reason, I proceeded with my search. I had not been searching more than thirty seconds when I came upon two male wedding bands in the console of his car. I picked them up and they seemed identical except for the fact that one was engraved on the inside. One of the bands I recognized to be the one that I had given to Dan on his fiftieth birthday. It was to replace his original band, which had been stolen years before. I did not have an opportunity to read what was engraved on the inside of the other wedding band. I was so focused and absorbed in what I was discovering that I was totally unaware of Dan's presence standing by the car. As I was about to read what was engraved on the wedding band, Dan promptly snatched both rings out of my hand and put them in his pants pocket. All I could say to him was, "Oh, so you are married to the whore now?" I thought to myself that I just uttered some real nonsense. Dan did not even bother to honor my question with an answer.

He just petitioned me, "Would you please stop searching my car, my briefcase, and all my stuff?"

I answered, "When you get rid of the whore, I will stop searching."

Needless to say, by the time we arrived at the house for the party the mood had been completely ruined for me. I remained puzzled as to the reason for the wedding band since Dan and I were not only still married, but also still living under the same roof. I knew by this time that you were aware, beyond the shadow of a doubt, that Dan was married and living with his wife and children. Why would he have a second wedding band? You are writing him e-mails, signing them "your wife," and proceeding to tell him in the e-mail that no one can come between the two of you and you are committed to him. All this with someone else's husband? It made me question what kind of person you are. None of this made any sense to me, or anyone else for that matter.

A few years later when you joined Facebook, you put your wedding day as February 14, 2007. How is that possible when Dan and I never divorced until April 28, 2011? When I think of all these situations that disrupted my life and caused me and my children so much pain and heartache, it is amazing to me that I have the inner strength and ability to forgive the two of you. Dan was my husband and took his matrimonial vows with me. However, you, your sister, and Dan's boss did everything possible to destroy my marriage so in the end you could get what you wanted: my husband. Both of you are responsible for the destruction of my marriage. You and Dan are a good pair; you are both living a lie. When you can knowingly post your wedding day as February 14, 2007, you are deceiving all your friends and family with that lie. If you and Dan were married on that day then Dan was committing a crime of bigamy, with you as an accomplice. I am happy to see that I am not the only person who is confused. When you actually, supposedly got married in May 2011 and you posted that you were married, one of your friends on Facebook wrote: "Again or still?" I was very amused by that as you were not only confusing them, but you were also consciously deceiving them. That says a lot about your character.

Visit to DC

Dear Mistress Ali,

Our daughter Mia was accepted into a very prestigious program at the University of North Carolina in Chapel Hill. The plan that I made was to have her parents drive her down, spend the weekend there, and bring her back. I'd made the hotel arrangements for Dan and me. My thought was that we could take the opportunity to talk and see what direction our marriage was taking and what action we were going to take to get us there. I made a hotel reservation with check-in on Thursday, the twenty-fourth of May, through Saturday, the twenty-sixth of May. To my surprise, when I informed Dan about the hotel information he asked me to cancel it because he had planned on going alone. Because, as he claimed, he had to visit one of their other center locations in Virginia, he did not think I should accompany him. Again, even though I thought he was lying, I still had my pride and I had no intention of begging him to let me go with him. He claimed he was going to make his own hotel arrangements.

On Thursday morning, Dan and my daughter left for the trip. Dan told me he would call when he arrived and let me know the hotel where he was staying. When they arrived he did call but I missed his call, so he left me a message on the phone. The message said, "We arrived in DC awhile ago; I don't yet have a hotel. I will call you later."

I was dumbfounded as my daughter's event was in *North Carolina*, not Washington, DC (where you lived). That is a Freudian slip if I ever heard one. That told me that was his plan, to drop our daughter off for her three-day event and then go on up to Washington, DC, to be with you. Again, I had no proof, just my gut. For the entire weekend no one was able to contact Dan. Dan had developed a pattern that he was apparently unaware of. Every time he was with you he never ever answered his telephone. He would check in with us from time to time, but we could never reach him. In the past when my oldest daughter was trying to reach him and was unsuccessful she would call your number and leave a hostile message to have her dad call her. You never answered your phone either, yet somehow he would always call back within the next couple of minutes. How transparent.

Well, once Dan dropped our daughter off no one was able to contact him. It was a horrible three days for my family because my young daughter, thinking her dad was in North Carolina with her, tried to reach him. When she couldn't, she called me, crying. I was helpless and going out of my mind with the hate that began to fill my entire being. I was in Atlanta, my older children were in Hilton Head, South Carolina, my youngest child was in North Carolina by herself, and her dad was nowhere to be found. This was not the experience that my daughter envisioned. Even though she was physically safe at the school with the program facilitators, my daughter was worried that something must have happened to her dad. I tried to reassure her and comfort her from afar without telling her what I believed was the truth, which was that her dad dropped her off and headed to Washington, DC, to be with his mistress.

At one point I myself began to think maybe I was wrong about my suspicions and that maybe something did happen to him. I became frantic and decided to get the information for the center in Virginia and check with them to inquire what day and time they were expecting him. Upon reaching the center director, I identified myself and explained the situation and just wanted to know if Dan had already been there, and if not, what time they were expecting him. As I should have guessed, the center director had no idea what I was talking about; there were no plans, arrangements, or need for Dan's visit to the center. Once again I proved that my suspicions were right. Dan was lying about everything. At that point, I knew beyond a doubt that Dan was in Washington, DC.

Dan called me later that day and had the nerve to be angry because I called the center looking for him. Dan was okay with lying to me and my children; he just had a problem with others knowing. Dan ruined the weekend for all of us. My three older children had gone away together for the weekend but spent a lot of time calling their baby sister and worrying about her. This was in addition to them being worried about, but also being angry with, Dan. I was mostly angry as far as it concerned Dan. I was preoccupied with my worry and concern for my daughter and upset with myself for allowing Dan to convince me to stay back in Atlanta when all the other parents were there with their children.

After Dan returned, my older children had the same suspicions as I did about where he spent his weekend. A few days later, my oldest daughter called me and told me that she wrote an e-mail to you and sent it from her dad's e-mail. She was pretty upset about what he had done by leaving her sister in North Carolina alone and being out of communication with everyone. I told her not to send the e-mail, because, quite frank-ly, my daughter did not need to be in any kind of communication with you. But she did anyway. She got into Dan's e-mail and sent it from there. She felt if she sent it from her own e-mail it might go to your junk mail. She sent it from her father's e-mail to guarantee its proper delivery. Now that letter is just the tip of the iceberg concerning the effect your affair with Dan had on my children.

The other sad thing about that weekend was my eldest son celebrated his thirtieth birthday that Friday. Dan didn't even care enough to call and wish his son a happy birthday. For the first time in his life, his dad completely ignored his birthday. This is despite the fact that the week prior was Dan's birthday and my son not only wished him a happy birthday, but also came by and brought him a gift. I guess this was just some of the new and painful behaviors that Dan had begun to exhibit. This affair was not just affecting me, it was destroying our children mentally and emotionally too. This was a completely new person in our lives and I think we were all at a loss as to what happened to the husband and father we knew.

This is the e-mail my daughter sent:

From:
To:
Subject: *Can't Forgive*
Date: Thu, 07 Jun 2007 16:05:39 +0000

I am not trying to harass you in anyway but I have to try to reach someone because I am not getting through to my father and I don't want to bring anymore stress on my mother. Hopefully after reading this you can offer me the truth because that is what I am lacking most in this whole messy affair. I need to know what is the status of your relationship with my father. I ask that you do not try to protect him or offer me advise to stay out of grown folks business because I can't. I need the truth to give my life some stability, so I can move on. You left Washington and indirectly left my father or so he has said. Yet he walks around and behaves like a man still hiding a secret. We can never reach him, communicate with him or even talk to him without some kind of hassle. Memorial Day weekend he drove my 16 year old sister to visit a college and she couldn't get a hold of him for two days. He tried to explain the mishaps but the details are of no consequence, ultimately the bottom line still remains the same Mia (that's my sister's name) couldn't get in touch with him and she was alone in the city with no one else to help her except those that were miles away.

Side Note: Something like this would never have happened a few years ago. My father was one of the most dedicated, responsible and reliable people I knew. Somehow his relationship with you and perhaps the stress of the whole affair/the lies/ or the wife hating your guts, has changed him into a different person; and of course he can't see it but we do. No one can talk to him, or reach him not even his own siblings, not even God himself. At times I wondered if my dad was on drugs because he is so different, cold and careless and just plain distant and I am the closest to him. No amount of reasoning or talking can make him understand how badly he has affected me, my mother, and siblings.

Anyway back to the Memorial day issue, my father claims he has spoken to my sister and squared things away BUT, in private conversations with my sister she tells me how she is still hurt and angry at him. There is even a song on the radio right now called "Makes me wonder" by Maroon Five that she said reminds her of my father.

I am sure by now you are wondering by now where you fit into all this: well I will tell you. I feel like the affair that you and he had is ruining my life and ultimately my faith in marriages altogether. I am sure you think that your actions with my father are none of my business and inconsequential but allow me to shed light on how it has implicated me. I no longer trust my father, hence why I am infiltrated his email to see if he was still lying to me. I need proof that you two are no longer corresponding. I need proof that he wasn't with you on Memorial Day. I need the truth. Of course my actions this morning were futile because he covers his tracks better than a woman with a good weave. He deletes everything, locks up everything, and for what. I don't understand why he doesn't put everyone (especially me) out of our misery and be honest about the direction he wants his life to take. How hard is that to do? Either he wants to be with you or whatever woman he is now seeing or he wants my mother but he can't have both!!! I am tired of the excuses as to why he didn't answer his phone or why he needs to make an impromptu trip somewhere, or why he is out hanging with other people instead of mending the mess he created at home. I have told him repeatedly that I didn't care what problems he and my mother were having before, cheating doesn't make it any better. He could have chosen to get out of the marriage before getting involved with you, if things were so bad. That's what I would want my husband to do. I wish my father could have just given my mother the choice to leave, instead of stepping out on her behind her back. Cheating and bringing a third party into his life only made things worse. Now I am sure every time he sees my mother he is constantly comparing her to you, and that thought makes me sick. My mother and father may have had problems but she never cheated, she never tried to make things worse by hurting him with an affair.

This is all very hard to deal with. This is not the father I know and I can only assume that you are partly to blame for his new attitude. I do know he respects you though, and so perhaps you can offer him some real advice because I feel like I am on my way out of this relationship with my dad. I wish you could think of someone else for a change and be honest about everything, we deserve that…yeah I know we are "only his kids" but we still deserve the truth. My father's actions are coming in between my relationship with my husband because I am obsessed with the thoughts that my husband can do the same thing to me. My pregnancy has been tainted by constant drama and upset and I want it all to stop. I want to know if you and my dad are going to be together or if he plans to check back into this family, get some help and live out the rest of his years trying to be happy, trying to have a better relationship with his children/grandchildren. I am so paranoid that something is going to happen, either sickness or death that will resolve this solution for us since _____ doesn't have the balls too. I have asked him several times to just get a divorce, make something final and each time he keeps promising to fix things but he never does. He does nothing. He comes home everyday and watches tv, pretending that we no longer exist in his world. He didn't even call my brother for his 30th birthday. When I asked him why he didn't he claimed he forgot. Those kind of actions didn't bother my brother because he said he expected it but deep down I know it hurt him just as much as it hurt me to hear it. I am literally scared for my baby to be born because there is so much chaos in my family. All created by two parties. At least you made some kind of attempt to distance yourself from us, but my father continues to linger around with no real conclusion to his marriage with my mother. He has yet to offer up a concrete decision as to what he is going to do, when to me the answer is simple. DIVORCE or TRY TO WORK THINGS OUT. How hard is it to make a decision. Only cowards sit by and do nothing, and it makes me wonder how he expects it to end. Will he die before this can be resolved. Will something happen to my mom due to all the stress she is under, only to leave me hating him for taking my mother away. I have no answers. I have asked him for answers and gotten nothing, now I am asking you. I know he is in Washington right now, and I know he is probably with you. This is what I believe and I could be way off but my heart tells me he is. My father exhibits all the signs of a man "caught up" so to speak. Why can't either of you be honest about things. Your lies are only making things worse for everyone. We are all adults and therefore can handle the truth. Do you think that after all the drama you helped create it is really unfair for me ask you to shed some light into what is going on? Do you really think that you are above all this mess and have no involvement. If you do, then I envy you; you get to come and go as you please with no heartache, no thoughts keeping you up at night, no worry over your parents' health and what stress is doing to it. You get to move on, live out your life. I guess that's why you think your Sh!t don't stink but it does...all the way to my home, into my life, into my marriage, into my unborn baby's life, into my siblings life, into my mother's life.

The following weekend, apparently the Phi Kappa Alpha's fraternity's annual black and white ball was being held in Washington, DC. Of course, I only got this information at a later date when you posted pictures on the Internet and below one picture was the caption, "Dan, me, my dad and mom [at the] Fraternity's Annual Black and White Ball." Imagine, you are sleeping with my husband and my children's father and you have the nerve to post pictures on bebo.com with your parents and my husband for the world to see. You never stopped to think what this public display of immorality was doing to my children; there was no shame in your game.

Dan left for work on that Friday. His niece was at our house visiting from Trinidad, and when I got home that afternoon she told me, "Uncle Dan said he had to go away with his job for the weekend." I asked her if she knew where he went and she said, "He said he was going to DC."

I was immediately upset but had to put up a good front for my niece. When I picked up my daughter from school that afternoon she too told me that her dad went to Washington, DC. Apparently, I, the wife, was the only one in the house with no knowledge of his whereabouts. What that told me was that he had no intention of stopping what he was doing. I knew at that point I could not live like that anymore. I decided I will not address the situation until my niece left to go back home. When Dan came back from his weekend, he acted as if everything was fine and so did I.

My niece left to go back home a week or two later. Soon after she left Dan came and told me that he had to go out of town for one week to Virginia for work. Needless to say I was 100 percent sure that he was lying. I said nothing because I was already beginning to deal with the end of my marriage and at that moment I did not care. Dan left to go on his trip on Saturday, June 30, and returned Sunday, July 8. While Dan was gone his closet in our master bedroom was locked. With great creativity I successfully removed every item of clothing and shoes and a briefcase that was locked from the master bedroom into the guest bedroom, but not before getting pliers and breaking into his briefcase. There actually was nothing of importance or value in the briefcase. I moved his tie rack and everything else out of the closet without removing or breaking the padlock he had on the door.

When Dan returned from his trip and walked into the master bedroom where I was sitting on the bed reading, he took his keys out of his pocket and unlocked the lock on the closet. He removed the lock and opened the door, only to find that his bare closet resembled Old Mother Hubbard's cupboard. He flew into a rage.

When I said, "Your new address is across the hall," he started to talk very loudly and threatened to leave and started to lie, swearing he was away for his job and he knew what I was thinking. I sat on the bed, silent, and pretended to be reading, which infuriated him even more. He walked across to the guest bedroom, where everything was completely set up and organized, up to and including his chest of drawers. When he saw the destruction of his lock on his briefcase, he came back in the room and threatened to call the police. I continued to ignore him, and believe it or not, he really called the police. I guess he called and said it was a domestic dispute.

To my shock and utter dismay the police did come to the house. I called my family in Florida to let them know what was going on. I could not believe this was happening, not in my house, not to me, not my husband. I felt as though I was about to break and fall apart and then I thought of my young daughter and took hold of my emotions. I acted as though it was an everyday occurrence for your husband of thirty-something years to call the police to your home because you broke the lock on his briefcase.

While the police were there, my son returned home from work and got quite a panic attack when he pulled in the driveway and saw two police cars in front of his home. Needless to say, when he heard what it was about he became very angry and told his dad that he hated him for what he was doing to the family and especially to his mom. The police officer told him that I did not commit a crime. Since we were married, what was his was also mine and what is mine was his; basically, I destroyed my own property. I think that was the moment my younger son changed his feelings and behavior toward his dad. I cannot imagine what Dan wanted the police to do. Did he want them to arrest me? I cannot help but feel that he was disappointed that they did not. I could be wrong, but that is how I felt.

That was the breaking point for me and the drama with you, Mistress Ali. I felt such hatred toward Dan that I spent the next six months cursing him, disrespecting him, and calling you—his mistress—the most vulgar names. I cried, screamed, yelled, had asthma attacks, and visited the emergency room often. My blood pressure was out of control; I did not care. With all my family living in Florida, I felt so alone. I attempted to act like I had everything under control for my children's sake. I stifled my tears until I was in the shower where no one could hear me.

I would go to work every day afraid that you or your sister would call and expose the drama that was unfolding in my life and in my home. Few people apart from my siblings and a few close friends knew what was happening in my life at the time. I cried in my car on my way to work, from work, in the shower, whenever I was alone. I prayed a lot and asked God to give me strength. I prayed and asked God to please keep me in good health as I was worried about getting a stroke or heart attack and leaving my children with a dad whom they felt was already dead. I spent time alone praying and crying. When Dan was around I spent my time crying and cursing. I felt like I did not know who I was anymore. I felt like I was losing my grip on reality, but I had to be strong for everyone else. I could not afford to let my children see me cry or be weak. I felt it would ruin them if they thought I was falling apart.

Trip to Florida

July 2007

Dear Mistress Ali,

In July Dan called me and said, "When I leave work this afternoon, I am going to Florida to visit my brother."

I began work at 4:30 a.m. and my youngest daughter was not comfortable with being in the house by herself when I left at 3:40 a.m. I asked Dan if he was taking Mia with him.

He explicitly answered, "No, she did not want to go."

I debated, "Since when does she get to decide what she does? Unless she plans on being home alone since I have to work in the morning."

Dan avoided the issue. "I have to go. I will call you back."

When I came off the phone with him I went and asked Mia why it was that she did not want to go to Florida with her dad and I told her she would have to go because I had to work in the morning. After some more discussion with her she informed me that her dad had never asked her about going. She said on the previous Sunday after church he told her he was going to Florida the next weekend. When Dan called to tell me that he was going to Florida after work, my first thought was that he was lying as usual and he was probably going out for a weekend with you. I decided that Mia was going with him. If he refused to take her, then I would know he was lying, but if he took her then he was speaking the truth. I called Dan back but his phone kept going to voicemail.

The night before he had informed me that the center where he worked was having a field trip and they were taking the students to Six Flags. I called him two more times and again it went to voicemail. The third time I decided to call the center and leave a message with the operator. When the operator answered the phone, I identified myself and asked if my husband was back from the park with the students. To my surprise the operator informed me that my husband did not come to work that day. I could not believe that Dan was up to his lies again, so I decided to call the bank and check on his debit card purchases.

The first transaction was at a Jiffy Lube, apparently for an oil change. The second transaction was for gas purchased in Tallahassee, Florida. I could not believe what I was hearing. I realized that when Dan called me the first time and explained that when he left work that afternoon he was going to Florida to visit Ben (his brother) he was already in Florida. I had Mia call her uncle and ask if her dad was there. I really expected to hear that he was not and that his brother was not expecting him.

Yet, again to my surprise, Dan was already there. I was confused because I wondered why, if he was really just visiting his brother, he wouldn't take Mia with him. I just assumed that if Dan was visiting his brother and his family there was no need to lie, there was no need to make me think he was at work when he wasn't. There was no need to say when he left work he was going to Florida when he was already in Florida. I just began to assume that he was a compulsive liar, because it seemed to me that he was lying for no reason. I was close to his brother for over thirty years and I loved him and his family, so there was absolutely no reason for Dan to lie.

Once I heard Dan really was there, I let it go. I did not bother to speak with him or make a fuss about why he felt the need to lie and why he did not take Mia. I guess I was still in a state of denial because I later learned that you were, in fact, with Dan at my in-laws' home that weekend. I then understood the reason for his lies and why he could not take his daughter.

You like to appear as a victim and pretend you did not know that Dan was married. Even if I gave you the benefit of the doubt and believe you did not know in the beginning, you absolutely knew that when Dan left your home, voluntarily, he came back home to try to make his marriage work. Yet you never gave us a chance. You knew that after your weekend in Florida Dan was returning to his home. The only thing accomplished by your visit with Dan to see my in-laws was the breaking of relationships. I stopped speaking to my brother- in-law; my children stopped speaking to their uncle.

Fortunately, my sister-in-law turned you guys away when you asked to stay at her home. The sad part about you and Dan, other than causing me pain and heartache, was that neither of you cared about the destruction you guys were causing in the family. Two grown people over fifty years of age in an immoral, illicit relationship, and both with jobs, could you please explain why you would not pay to stay in a hotel? You decided to take your trips and then put innocent people in those awkward positions. Clearly you were unaware that Dan's family and I have never had any problems over all these years. Now my sons still do not speak to their uncle. I do not have the same relationship with my brother-in-law even though I speak to him now. I do not have the relationship with Dan's niece as I used to have; my children do not have the same relationships with their uncle and cousins as they had in the past, all because of you, Mistress Ali, and Dan.

Thanksgiving & Christmas

Dear Mistress Ali,

Between August and November of the same year Dan had mysterious trips, and according to him they were always due to his job. Sometimes he said nothing at all and my children and I would be expecting him home on a Friday afternoon, but he just would not show and we would call him on his phone and there would never be an answer. That would be our clue that he was with you. In November I cancelled the Thanksgiving celebration with my family for the second time. I was not happy and I chose to stop playing games of make-believe. I called my family members and I told them I would not be hosting Thanksgiving.

My daughter decided to have her parents and siblings over as she was already entertaining her in-laws. Because of the strained relationship I had with Dan, I did not want to make things unpleasant. I had the option to work, so I decided to work so Dan could spend Thanksgiving with his children, his new granddaughter, his son-in-law, and his children. I was okay with my decision and had already discussed it with my children and they were all okay with it. Well, it was not long into my shift that my older daughter, Simone, called to say that her dad was not there. I was at work, so I had no knowledge of what was going on, so I had no answers for her.

I received a call about a half hour later from my youngest daughter, Mia, who was upset and crying because her dad was not there and he was not answering his phone. Well, I must tell you that was the worst eight hours I'd ever worked. My oldest daughter was sad, mad, and embarrassed because dinner was ready to be served and her in-laws kept waiting and waiting for Dan to arrive; he never showed. My younger daughter, already emotional that her cousins and family were not there for Thanksgiving, as was the custom, was ten times more upset and emotional that her dad did not come and I was not there because I chose to work. I never would have chosen to work if I had known that Dan was not going to show up. Of course, my son, Kyle, who lived at home, said that as soon as I left for work his dad left the house. Kyle did not go over to his sister's house for another two hours. When he got there he was surprised to learn that his dad was not there and of course no one knew where he was. Dan never returned home until the Friday night after Thanksgiving. We all later learned that you were in Georgia and entertaining for the holiday.

The interesting thing that happened for me on Thanksgiving Day, apart from the pain and sadness I felt for my children, I had a feeling of calm and acceptance that the marriage was over. The reason I accepted that position then was because prior to Thanksgiving I had felt that whatever Dan's reason for having an affair and fracturing our marriage was, I felt that part of the blame had to lie with me, even though I did not know what. I felt that whatever Dan's reasons were in his mind, I could direct them back to me. The saddest part of that unfortunate, unhappy Thanksgiving was what Dan did to his children. His behavior was inexcusable, wicked, and unforgivable. These were our children who had done nothing to him. They were the only people in the world who Dan should love unconditionally. For Dan to hurt them so terribly, for no reason, made me accept the fact that no matter what lies Dan may have told you or anyone who would listen about why his marriage was broken, it had nothing to do with me and everything to do with Dan. You gave him a good reason. After that day, I knew that it was just a matter of time before it would all come to an end.

December of that year, with Christmas approaching, Dan decided to inform me that he was not going with us to Florida as we had done for the past seventeen years.

I said to him, "If you do not go with us, I hope you will be gone by the time we get back."

Dan defended, "I do not want to go for Christmas, but when you all come back I want us to work at fixing our marriage in the New Year."

I told Dan that if he did not go with us for Christmas there was nothing to work on in the New Year. He told me that he was going to have a discussion with the children and let them know what he decided. I told him if he was going to tell the children about his plan to stay in Georgia and not go to Florida, expect them to be upset.

A few days later I had an asthma attack and went to the emergency room. When I returned home, Dan called Mia and told her about his plan to remain in Georgia for Christmas. Mia became very upset and said to Dan, "If you don't come to Florida for Christmas, do not ever speak to me again." This was all said with pain and tears and lots of emotion.

I guess Dan, as usual, only thinking about himself, began to reprimand Mia for what she said. Mia, with her recent memories of Thanksgiving, was unbending and began to argue with Dan about his decision to be absent for Christmas. I guess Dan had enough of her hysteria, so he shut the door in her face.

Mia being emotional, frustrated, and upset, screamed, "Daddy!" and kicked the door.

Dan immediately opened the door and slapped her in the face. That was the first time in her seventeen years that her dad had ever laid a hand on her and she went completely out of control, screaming and crying. My two sons ran upstairs when they heard the screaming. Just then Dan raised his hand to slap her again and my oldest son got in between them, put his two palms on Dan's chest, and pushed him back into the room.

What happened next was shocking and insane. Dan did the most unbelievable thing. He reached into his bag and took out his gun. My daughter became hysterical and my younger son stood there in the hallway with his fists clenched and breathing heavily. Dan had his two hands behind his back holding the gun; he never pointed it at anyone, but I did not care. I knew at that point I had to do something before someone got hurt. I walked up to Dan and told him to put that gun away before I called 911, but he ignored me. I tried desperately to diffuse the nightmare by asking my oldest son to leave and take his brother with him. He was reluctant. I again begged Dan to put away the gun.

As I realized I had no control over these three men or my hysterical seventeen-year-old, I went back into my room then came back to ask Dan one more time. But again he ignored me. Before I could dial 911, Mia began to depress the panic buttons on the alarm keypad. I repeatedly put in the code to silence the deafening alarm, but she continued to press the buttons as it served for a great distraction to the men. I pleaded with Nick to go home and to take Kyle with him once the security company called and alerted me that police officials were on their way. I relayed this to the boys and assured them that we would be fine. They left. I called my older daughter; she was already on her way over.

The police arrived. I told them what was taking place and why they were called. They went upstairs to talk to Dan and Mia, and I went downstairs. My daughter arrived shortly after the police and we were sitting in the living room talking about what had happened when the police came downstairs with Dan in handcuffs. I asked the officer why he was arresting him; I did not know that was going to happen. The officer said that they had to take his gun and they could not take his gun without making an arrest. After speaking to Mia, the only thing the officers charged Dan with was simple battery for slapping her. Soon after the police left with Dan, my boys came back to the house and we sat in the living room in a state of complete shock. Not one of the five of us could even begin to understand what had just taken place.

My younger son, Kyle, said, "If I didn't know better, I would think that Dad is on drugs." That statement is a good indication of the different person that Dan had become.

I later found out that you were coming to Georgia for Christmas. It then became clear to me that I could not do this anymore. You could have him. You fought long and hard. The saddest thing I learned about you was while you were spending all this time cheating with my husband and causing havoc and pain and suffering in my family, you had problems of your own. Your daughter was screaming for your attention. She got into trouble with the law and became part of the system. Instead of leaving my husband and focusing on helping your daughter to feel special and loved, you devoted all your love and attention on a married man with a family of his own. I could not begin to understand the choices you made.

At the time of this incident I had been with Dan for thirty-five years, had four children with him, and I was not prepared to spend one more day in this drama, dragging my children through this dysfunction. You, on the other hand, had one daughter who needed you, but instead you would leave her in Maryland for Christmas to come to Georgia to be here with Dan. I could never be a mother like that. So if Dan wanted someone who would put him first, second, and third, above everything else, I supposed you were the right one. If I had a child involved with the justice system, she would be my priority and my only concern before any man, especially a man who is married, who is not even the father of my child.

The day after Dan's arrest, he called the house about twelve times, begging us to come and bail him out. I had no intentions of going as I was still sick with bronchitis. Kyle refused to go help him. He felt we should leave him there. However, Nick and Simone decided to take care of the situation and go and bail him out. They brought him home and he packed his stuff. He left without saying thank you to Nick and Simone or saying a word to Mia or myself. The following day he came back to the house and packed more of his things. He gave Nick a gas card and gave us some money as he knew we were leaving to go to Florida in a few days to spend Christmas there. Dan got his wish to spend Christmas with you, his mistress, but at the expense of his children, his friends, my family, his family, and everything that had been important to him during the course of his fifty-five years. Now he had his mistress and none of these things mattered.

Mia

Dear Mistress Ali,

I called Dan to inquire about his plans to get Mia to school since he had moved out. In the past he would take her to school and I would pick her up. Now that he was no longer living at home and I had to be at work at 4:30 a.m. that was a problem, but it was his problem. My eldest son gave up his apartment and moved back home to be there in the morning with Mia. My younger son worked nights and Mia did not want to be home alone when I left for work at 3:50 a.m.

At first Dan tried to act like that was my problem and how Mia got to school was not his issue. I threatened to call the Department of Family and Children's Services if Mia missed one day of school. I guess he did not want his child in the system, nor did he want any

97

more involvement with the police. He quickly arranged for Mia to meet him at a Toyota dealership, where he purchased a car for her so she could take herself to school. That worked for me because now it meant I did not have to pick her up after school either. Under different circumstances Mia would have been elated to have been given a vehicle at seventeen years old; that is the dream of every teenager. However, her car came with mixed emotions. This was her senior year and everything she'd known for seventeen years seemed to be changing. To her, her dad buying a car to take herself to and from school symbolized the point of no return for him coming back home.

Let me shed some light for you on who Mia was prior to the drama you and Dan created in my family and the utter devastation you created for her. I want to make this clear to you because when a woman becomes involved with a married man she thinks only of her pleasure and the man's. She tells herself she is loved, but she never stops to think of what she is doing to a wife and the children of that family as a whole. That love cannot be true when it is the cause of such pain for others.

Mia was our last child. When she was born our other children were thirteen, eleven, and six years of age. Mia was loved beyond words by her older siblings; she was considered a perfect child. I often joked with my older children and would tell them I kept trying until I got it right. This was all in good fun because they also thought that she was very special. At age six, Mia declared she was going to be a pediatrician when she grew up. We did not even know that she knew what that word meant, but when asked she stated it is the doctor that she goes to see all the time. Mia was an A student and honor roll student from the time she started attending school in the third grade after being homeschooled in her earlier years. The time between third grade and graduating from high school, Mia had several commendations that everyone was very proud of.

Apart from her exemplary classroom academic performance, Mia played the violin, opened a cake-making business, babysat for my friends' children, and even taught herself the alphabet in sign language while she sat in kindergarten class at age five. Her teachers assumed we taught her at home and we thought they taught her in school.

At the age of two and a half years old, Mia, who sucked her finger from birth, abruptly stopped without any help or direction from her parents because of a promise I made to her that if she stopped sucking her finger I would buy her a pair of Barney sneakers. (She loved Barney.) Even her pediatrician was impressed by that accomplishment because he said breaking the habit of finger sucking was a difficult task for parents to do. That showed, according to her doctor, the strong will and determination she possessed and told us as parents we should pray that she channeled that strong determination into positive things, which she did.

In elementary school, Mia participated in an essay competition titled "If I Were Mayor." Two thousand three hundred essays were submitted and eleven winners were selected from eleven congressional districts by a panel of city officials. Mia was the winner for Decatur. Each winner received a $250 savings bond and other prizes. The eleven winners were honored at a luncheon in Atlanta and the mayors from each of the winners' hometown and the president of the Georgia Municipal Association were also present at the luncheon.

That same year, Mia participated in an art competition held by the archdiocese of Atlanta. This was the Catholic Campaign for Human Development Youth Art Contest. Mia won first place. In addition to the monetary reward, winning the contest resulted in the transfer of copyright of her entry to the archdiocese of Atlanta, and her art submission was used as an educational tool about peace at conference exhibits and a variety of events. It was also used as a Catholic greeting card together with a prayer for peacemakers.

Mia also decided while in the sixth grade that she wanted to learn to knit. I bought her the needles and the yarn. I really do not know who taught her the first few stitches, but soon after I bought the materials Mia was knitting winter scarves and hats for her friends and her brothers and sisters. To this day, years later, whenever you find Mia, you might find her with her knitting needles and yarn and her population of clients has expanded to include nieces, nephews, and cousins.

The following year, Mia received a certificate of merit for participating in the twenty-third talent search conducted by Duke University talent identification program for mathematically and verbally gifted seventh-graders. During the same year, Mia applied and was accepted into the very competitive Ben Carson Science Academy for their summer program. The last sentence to her application essay was, "So if I could participate in this program I would be truly inspired to be just like Dr. Carson, an extraordinarily outstanding doctor in the medical field of Pediatrics." At the time of her acceptance into the program, Mia was thirteen years old.

Her dream continued. In middle school, Mia was accepted into the A Better Chance Program, or ABC program. A Better Chance, Inc. is the predominant national resource for identifying, recruiting, and developing leaders among young people of color—African-American, Latin, Asian-American, and Native Americans—in the United States. Through a unique assessment model, ABC refers academically talented students entering grades six through eleven to some of the nation's finest independent and public schools to be considered for placement and financial aid.

In her freshman year in high school, A Better Chance held the Goldman Sachs Institute for Entrepreneurial Thinking National Business Plan competition. Mia participated in this competition using her cake-baking business, which she had begun in the fourth grade. As Mia grew older her cakes began to be more creative and specialized. The Goldman Sachs Institute for Entrepreneurial Thinking is an entrepreneurship program for A Better Chance scholars and recent alumni. The applicants engaged in the ME, Inc. program, a mini ABA course designed to develop leadership and entrepreneurial skills. The scholars gained personal development skills like goal setting, time management, and marketing oneself for greater college and marketing success. They also gained real-world business skills in personal finance, business development, and social advancement.

At the conclusion, the students had to create a business plan based on their life goals. For Mia, this was to own a bakery on the side, all the while maintaining her dream of becoming a physician. After the Atlanta regional competition was held, Mia won first place. She received $500 and an all-expense paid trip to New York, together with her parents, to compete in the national competition. Mia was the youngest student to participate in the New York competition that year and received a certificate for her outstanding performance at the Goldman Sachs Institute for Entrepreneurial Thinking National Business Plan competition in New York, New York.

In high school Mia continued to have academic success while doing volunteer work with Hosea Feed the Hungry. She also volunteered at Horizon's summer camp teaching minority students. She was involved in flag line, track, and Spanish club as her extracurricular activities. Outside of school, she was a member of the W. E. B. Dubois Society of Atlanta and was an extraordinary minister of holy communion. Her senior year of high school, she volunteered to be a part of a program to mentor freshman students.

In the beginning of her junior year, Mia's school counselor and teachers chose to enroll her in advanced placement courses. This was the same time I discovered your affair with Dan. To this day, the most painful part of what you and Dan caused in my life is the destruction of my daughter's dreams. I felt a certain amount of guilt for my part in the constant arguments, verbal assaults, and rage that I demonstrated toward Dan. I did not focus on my children as I had done in the past. I did not observe what was happening to Mia and how it was affecting her. I was too consumed with my own pain and anger.

Even when Mia told me that she was beginning to struggle in school and she tried reaching out to me for help, I was not there for her, emotionally or mentally. I regret that every day of my life. I was in such a dark place at the time that unfortunately the only thing I was focused on was Dan and you and my marriage. I seemed physically, mentally, and emotionally unable at that period in time to be the mother that I had been my entire life.

The result of all the drama had long-lasting effects on Mia and her dreams. Although Mia was successful in being accepted into two great universities, University of Miami and Clemson University, her lifelong dream had been to get into Yale. Prior to the situation that began in her junior year that had not been an unrealistic dream. A part of the application process for both of the universities where she was accepted was an essay. I was thrilled that she was accepted at both of these schools, but when I read the essay that she submitted with her application I was very sad. I had no clue how to fix her and help her with her pain. The following is the essay that Mia submitted to the universities that helped her gain acceptance into both schools. (She chose Clemson, Go Tigers!)

Augustine Naper said, "In each family a story is playing itself out, and each family's story embodies its hope and despair." In my family's story, I'm the main character. And I feel that with my role written out of the story as I leave for college, this story will end. The antagonist is, unfortunately, my father. The setting is a not quite broken home and the other characters are my 2 older brothers, older sister, and mother. Sadly, there is no director yelling, "Lights! Camera! Action!" or even better, "Cut." This is not planned and there is no script. The people and the drama are real, yet so are the tears and the emotional pain.

The first scene starts as a flashback to the childhood years of my siblings and I. Interactions between us and my father were limited, a foreshadowing of the future. The best image of a father only portrayed in the presence of others. It was the making of how my mother refers to him now, the world's best politician. Therefore, the memories don't account for much. My mother reminds me how at six years old, I asked my father why he only laughed when people were around. Even as a young and naïve child, my words spoke volumes, yet apparently not enough to get through to my father. Constantly nit picking, as our story progresses, we would come to learn it was because of insecurities. Yet these insecurities didn't change the pain and anger caused so easily and so often.

The second scene starts with more recent events which build the rising action of our story. Maybe my father didn't know there are no retakes. The level of apathy for his immoral actions is baffling to family, friends, and counselors. Yet in addition to his apathy, all my mother's attempts to reconcile the situation have been thwarted by his silence, making the situation worse. Because of this, I fear that my leaving will cause the climax, and perhaps, my family's breaking point. I am the rope holding my family together, each person holding on for one reason: me. And without this common ground to stand on, I fear my home will come tumbling down to the ground. The remainder will be a divided family, yet their affection towards me will be multiplied as compensation for the hardships.

Sometime during the summer of 2008, Dan called Mia and said to her, "Do not call me for the next five to six days as I will be unavailable." That was the extent of his conversation. Mia did not ask him any questions since he had, by this time, become very secretive, or he gave information that was usually a lie. Mia concluded that her dad was in the airport when he spoke to her because she heard a flight announcement being made in the background while he was on the phone with her. At this time, Dan's residence was your home in Atlanta, which he shared with your sister. The only means for his four children to communicate with him was his cell phone or work phone since no one knew where he was living except me, due to my investigative work. No one had any other phone number for him.

Dan did not care if there was an emergency with one of his children (which there had been), if one of his family members got sick, if my mother and his mother-in-law of thirty-three years passed away as she had been ill for two weeks prior to his call to Mia. He could not be reached and no one knew where he was. The only thing that we all knew with certainty was that he had to have been with you. Once Dan was with you, he was disconnected from any and all members of his family. Usually he just wouldn't answer his phone, but this time he gave Mia advance notice not to call him. She was the only one of his four children that he was communicating with at the time, and it surely did not appear to bother him in the least. It did not bother him that for six days no one knew where he was or could reach him in case of an emergency.

This behavior was always upsetting and painful to our children as it made them feel abandoned by their dad. They felt that the only person who mattered to him was you. Though I am sure that was your heart's desire, what kind of person must you be to condone that behavior in a man with a family and children?

Well, two weeks after Dan returned from his six-day disappearing act my mother did in fact pass away. Dan was called and informed of my mother's passing by one of my siblings, who was Dan's best friend. That evening Dan came to the house, I suppose to offer his condolences to me and check on Mia and Kyle. Dan did not stay at the house very long, but in the short time he was there he managed to cause me more emotional distress in addition to the empty feeling from the loss of my mother.

It was clear to us at that point that during the six days he could not be reached he had been in Aruba on vacation with you, his mistress. He did not let anyone know where he was during those six days, but on the day my mother died he came to the house bearing gifts; two gifts were for his granddaughter and one for Mia. He bought a t-shirt for my granddaughter that read "Someone who loves you very much went to Aruba and bought you this t-shirt." The other gift was a little jumper with a headband and read "Grandma's Little Princess." I could not believe your gall, to refer to yourself as a grandma to my precious granddaughter when all you were at that time was Dan's mistress.

The day of my mother's memorial in Florida was, unfortunately, the same day that Mia was to move into her dorm. The university was kind enough to allow her to move in three days earlier. Dan made no effort whatsoever to be there for his daughter or to assist her, so my son Kyle and I did what was necessary to help her with the move. I should have been in Florida at that time with my siblings, assisting with the preparation of my mother's memorial service and funeral, but because of Dan's refusal to help I had to stay in Georgia to take care of the situation with Mia. When a child leaves home to go away to college, it is a very difficult time for the child and the parents. Mia's time was made even more difficult because of her grandmother's passing and her father's refusal to help with her transition. Dan flew to Florida for the memorial service and flew back to Georgia the same day. Mia had to return to school on Sunday to start school on Monday. I was supposed to be accompanying my siblings to Trinidad to bury our mom.

While in Florida I asked Dan if he could take Mia to school on Sunday, but he refused. As a result, I had the difficult task of flying back to Georgia after the memorial service to drive Mia to school, drive back to Georgia, then fly back to Miami to join my siblings on the flight to Trinidad for my mom's burial. The behavior that Dan exhibited certainly contradicted the behavior of the person that I had known all those years. When I took Mia to school on Sunday it was a day of unbelievable sadness and emotional turmoil for both her and me. Leaving for college and losing her grandmother was sad enough, but having to experience the feeling of abandonment by her father was nothing short of catastrophic.

I went to Trinidad to bury my mother the day after I took Mia to school. I returned three days later. Upon my return to Georgia and my arrival at my home later that night, I attempted to call my siblings in Florida to let them know I was home but I discovered that my phone had been disconnected because Dan had made the decision not to pay the bill. I was hurt, depressed, and angry, all due to the fact that Dan was just cruel to do that to me while he was paying bills in your home. My cell phone did not work very well in my home, so that night I lay in bed and had a complete meltdown. My mother had passed, my daughter had gone away to school, my cheating husband was now living at your house and not paying bills in mine, and I could not even speak to my family or friends because I had no phone service. I cried uncontrollably for what seemed like hours and I felt completely alone.

The next morning I woke, drove my car to the Publix parking lot where I had very good reception on my cell phone, and I called you and threatened you by promising to call your boss and your co-workers and let them know all about you and Dan. I told you if Dan should cut any more of my utilities again I would call your boss and his boss and expose you both. Clearly that worked, because for one year following that conversation Dan paid the bills without a problem.

Another example of Dan abandoning his children. When Mia started school, her fees and meal plan needed to be paid. Dan would not even take part in a discussion because he did not want her to attend that school; his standards for her were much lower. That was very stressful and heartbreaking for Mia because she worked very hard to get into the university. Unfortunately, if you and Dan had not exposed her to your affair and the drama that came with it, I guarantee you Mia would have received a full scholarship to the university of her choice. I took the funds from my 401K to pay the portion of her tuition that was not paid for by financial aid and her meal plan of $1,500 was paid for by one of our closest, dearest friends.

In November of this same year, everyone at my company was either laid off or had to relocate in order to keep their job. This created a lot of anxiety and depression for Mia because at the time of the situation at work I had been on medical leave due to my declining health caused by all I was trying to cope with. Within a nine-month period, my husband abandoned me and my children, he had taken out a gun on his children, my last child went away to college, my mother passed away, my health declined, and I had no job to return to. This was a lot to deal with for me and it was ten times harder for Mia, who felt that her life had been turned upside down. Getting $10 from her dad was a battle, and I was on disability. Eventually Mia decided to get two jobs to maintain some semblance of financial stability throughout her remaining years at college, which was a bad idea.

By the end of Mia's freshman year, not surprisingly, it was not a successful year for her academically. This was the same child with all the self-motivation, ambition, and drive who developed a vision of what her career path was going to be since she was six years old. She had a bright future to be whoever she wanted to be and do whatever she wanted to do. For the first time in her nineteen years, she had to experience failure.

Good parents do everything in their power to prevent their children from experiencing failure. Children sometimes take that path, regardless of what their parents say or do, because they are not always focused and mature. That is somewhat expected in raising children. What is not expected, however, is when parents are blessed with a child like Mia. In such a case, it is unconscionable that a parent could be so selfish to be only thinking of his needs, all the while undermining his child's progress. This is exactly what Dan did to his daughter, with your help, of course.

I feel partly responsible as I was dealing with my own issues inflicted by you two as well. Yet what was sad about this situation was that Mia had always defined who she was by being successful at everything she did, but now this failure changed who she was. It seemed that she lost her self-confidence and became depressed. I tried as best as I could to comfort and encourage her. I asked her sister, my sister, and my brother to speak with her and encourage her to believe that she still had the intelligence to succeed. I decided to send her to therapy again when she came home for the summer in the hopes that she would be in a much better place by the beginning of her sophomore year. I hoped and prayed that things would be different by then. They were not.

Just as we were working through and discussing the rocky year she had, she received a letter from school that completely destroyed her. The following letter set back all the progress we felt we were making with her.

May 12, 2009

Dear Ms.   :

Thank you for your application for financial aid for the 2009-10 academic year at Clemson University. Unfortunately, we are unable to offer you any financial assistance at this time due to your failure to maintain satisfactory academic progress. This denial of aid is based on policies defined in the University's financial aid publication as required by federal regulations.

This annual review was conducted at the end of spring semester. If you had extenuating circumstances which contributed to your failure to maintain satisfactory academic progress, you may submit a letter of appeal to the Financial Aid Appeals Committee. If you plan to attend summer school, please submit your appeal after completion of coursework.

Please note that satisfactory progress is separate and distinct from continuing enrollment requirements. The decision and appeal process for satisfactory progress is the responsibility of the Financial Aid Office while continuing enrollment issues are the responsibility of the Office of Undergraduate Academic Services.

If you have questions regarding the University's satisfactory academic progress standards, please refer to the policy found at www.clemson.edu/finaid/SAP.htm.

Sincerely,

Director of Financial Aid

STUDENT FINANCIAL AID OFFICE
G-01 Sikes Hall   Box 345123   Clemson, SC 29634-5123
864.656.2280   FAX 864.656.1831

111

Mia knew enough to know what GPA was expected of her in order to be accepted in medical school. She had researched all that information since before she entered high school, so that letter thoroughly devastated her. She felt that if she could not even remain in school then all her dreams and hopes were gone.

I tried talking to and reassuring her, praying and everything else I could think to do for my child. Somewhere along the way what I had been saying to her finally registered. I said, "Do not let other people decide your future. No matter what happens, you do not give up. You just work harder to achieve your goals. It would be worth it in the end."

Thank God Mia had a sister like Simone who loved and believed in her. She talked to Mia, and between the both of us Mia decided that she was not going to be put out of school. She wrote the following letter...

To Whom It May Concern:

I received your letter dated May 12, 2009 regarding the denial of my application for financial aid due to my "failure to maintain satisfactory academic progress." I am very grateful for the opportunity given to me to appeal this decision. I am happy that the year 2008 is over as it will forever be what a year to remember as my worst year ever. This is due to a number of reasons.

First and foremost, my happy home that consisted of my two brothers, sister, and both my parents came tumbling down upon my discovery that my father who was happily married to my mom (or so we all thought), was having an affair. My dad left the home on January first to move in with his mistress. Lest we forget, my parents were married at that time for 33 years. My dad was the head of the household in every way especially financially. Yet, even thought he had moved out, he continued to support the home 100% until I—the last child living at home—moved out to go to college. It was as if my father had died and was replaced with this other person in his body. To this day, my dad is unrecognizable to anyone who knew him before. In august, when I left to come to Clemson, my dad refused to assist with anything financially or otherwise related to my attending college. This situation put a sever strain on my mom who, in the 33 years of her marriage, only worked part time for a total of 13 years. The last 11 of her years were spent at Air Canada when I started school at age 8 after being home-schooled. On the 11th of August, the week anticipating the week of my moving into my dorm in Clemson, my grandmother—my mom's mom—passed away. It was a large stressor to receive permission from the wonderful staff of Clemson's housing department to move in on the Thursday before move in that Saturday, August 16. This was because my grandmother's funeral was scheduled for the same Saturday.

Not only was I an emotional wreck for having been separated from my high school friends, but now I had also lost my dad and my grandmother. And what was even more stress was that I felt as if I was losing my mother as well. My mom is pretty strong on the outside, which I have since learned was merely an image she portrayed to make things seem okay for my siblings and I. However, all this began to have a serious affect on my mother's health. My mother's asthma began to flare up, which was very unusual since she had had her asthma under control since about 2000. My mother's visits to the doctor also began to increase to almost weekly because on October 30th, she had been diagnosed with —the silent killer—high blood pressure, depression, anxiety, and constant migraines. Because of all of this, my mother was sent home from work by her doctor and placed on sick leave for 3 to 6 months.

In august my mother took a hardship withdrawal from her 401k to pay for my remaining fees. In November, one my mom's friends, a close family friend, paid for my meal plan and bought the remainder of things I would need for my time in college because my mother couldn't afford it. In January, my mother took out the remainder of her 401k to pay for my spring semester and my mother's sister and two of my maternal cousins combined paid for my meal plan.

As if we did not have enough problems, on November 3rd, Air Canada, where my mom worked for the past 11 years, laid off all of their employees and replaced them with a contracted company. My mother was given two choices: move to Los Angeles (which was impossible for a number of reasons) or take early retirement. Early retirement will only give her a check for $300.00 per month starting in July of this year.

The only thing that matters to me and gives me hope and something to strive for right now is being able to attend Clemson. I did better in my spring semester in spite of all that was still going on. I am very much like my mother in that what doesn't kill me only makes me stronger. And I would love to have an opportunity this year to really prove myself and how strong I have become. My dad has completely abandoned my family now and moved to Maryland. Believe it or not, this makes it easier for my family. With my dad filing for divorce, there is a temporary court order for my dad to continue to pay the mortgage and the bills until the divorce is finalized. My mom's best friend paid for an attorney for my mother and my older siblings are helping as best they can to restore things to create a "new normal" for ourselves.

I am begging whoever is responsible for making this decision to pleas allow me this one year to attend Clemson without cost to allow my mom to get back on her feet and get a job. My mom is still in therapy and her health is slowly, but surely, improving. Ergo, I certainly do not have any desire to add to her depressed mental state by not being able to return to school. It had been a horrible year but things are getting better. Please find it in your hearts to have some compassion for me. I had been in therapy, but was unable to go when I was in school—even though that was when I needed it the most. However, I am going now. Everything I have told you here can be proved with supporting documents, if you wish. Thank you again for the opportunity to explain what my therapist and I considered to be extenuating circumstances which contributed to my failure to maintain satisfactory academic progress.

Going away to college, being away from my home and family was hard enough without the ongoing drama that my dad and his mistress created for my mother and my family. I still love and miss my dad but I am doing fine without him. My brothers, who in a way have replaced my dad, are there to support me at all times. Also my sister, brother-in-law, and mother are there too.

I am looking forward to hear from you and I hope it will be positive. If it is necessary for my therapist to write a letter on my behalf, it will not be a problem, if that will help as well.

Thank You,

Our prayers were answered. Mia was able to return to university in the fall and begin her sophomore year. Mia decided that her plans for medical school would have to be delayed. She was aware that her only chance of acceptance would depend on the score on the MCAT. She made a decision that upon graduation she would take a year or two off and study in order to give herself a chance. The remainder of her years at the university continued to be a struggle, having to work two jobs while attending school in order to survive. Her life would have been so much better if her dad and you had not created this mess and drama in our lives. All I can do is hope and pray that when Mia does apply to medical school that she is given an opportunity to explain her unacceptable GPA and does get accepted in one of the schools she plans to apply to. This way her dream can still be attained.

Our Conversation

Dear Mistress Ali,

In November of 2008, I called you again out of frustration to tell you about the destruction you and Dan were creating for my family. I don't know if you recall that conversation, but I complained that while Dan was paying bills in your home in Lilburn, his daughter was going without. One of the things you said to me in that conversation was, "I don't take care of no man."

I took that to mean he was going to pay his way while you all were together and you really did not care about his finances. The conversation was very civilized. Looking back, years later, I guess I had to have been in a desperate, dark place. I remember telling you a bit about my past life with Dan, my children, and how long we had been together (among other things). I remember telling you that after I had packed Dan's stuff and he left our home that I never ever asked him to come back home; he did that on his own. And in spite of that you still continued your relationship with him. I also told you that the first time Dan left home and moved in with you he came back to our home every day and we did not know why. I also didn't understand how you could have him living in your home while he was coming to my home every day even though I was not even speaking to him. Lastly, how desperate you must have been to put up with that.

You then told me that Dan told you I had moved out of the home and left our fifteen-year-old daughter in the home by herself and that was the reason he had to come by the house every day. Well, I told you then, and I will now take the opportunity to tell you again, that was another of his big lies. I *never* left my children ever. I have been the only parent who put our children first, obviously.

I guess you believed Dan because, first, you wanted to believe him, and secondly you assumed that I was the kind of mother that you were. You had a very troubled daughter, desperate for the guidance and support of a woman and mother. In an effort to get your attention, she did a lot of things that caused her to be in juvenile detention and group homes. She ran away from the group home and came back to your home in Lilburn. What did you do? You called the police and had them pick her up as you refused to keep her in your home. On her sixteenth birthday she was looking forward to seeing you at the group home. Well, that was the very same weekend that Dan rented the car and lied about it because you two were going to visit your daughter five hours away. Could you not have devoted some time alone with your daughter instead of taking your married lover with you?

I think kids do stupid things sometimes for attention and your daughter was screaming for yours. It is a pity that you did not hear her and devote your time to being a better mother instead of a great mistress. Dan did not care one bit about your daughter; he barely cared about his own. I think you and Dan are a perfect couple and are well suited for each other. He put his children last and, for her remaining time, you continuously put your daughter last.

Back to the conversation you and I had. I remember in that conversation you inquired, "Could I ask you a question?"

I said, "Go ahead because this will be the last time you will have this opportunity."

"Did Dan ever ask you for a divorce?"

And I proclaimed, "No, he did not, and let me make this clear to you, I will never divorce Dan. And if you are waiting for me to divorce Dan, that will never happen."

There was a silence on your end, so I went on, "If Dan wants a divorce he can go ahead and file, but I would never file." I reiterated, "The only way that Dan and I would be divorced is if he goes and files."

I suppose by you asking me that question I assumed he must have lied to you about that also but never thought that you and I would ever talk, so he was free to lie as he assumed you would never know the truth. Dan being a liar was obviously not something that bothered you. Even though you told me early in the drama that you did not know he was married, based on the information that your sister wrote me in her e-mail, she claimed that Dan gave you "many scenarios" about his marital status. In other words, he told you several lies from the very beginning but despite that you pursued the relationship. As I told you before, I have pride. I could never be that desperate.

Shortly after that conversation between you and me, I was served with divorce papers early one morning. I have to assume that you initiated the paperwork because of your question to me on the phone and something even more obvious. One thing about Dan is he had a great memory for dates and numbers. In the thirty-six years we were together, he never forgot our anniversary, he never forgot my birthday or our children's. However, the date of our marriage was incorrect in the divorce application, something Dan would know. You are pretty pathetic and a fraud.

In January, the second semester for Mia began and again there was no support from Dan. So again I had to take money out of my 401K. In addition to which, thanks to my sister and two of my nephews, we all contributed to make the $1,500 payment for her meal plan, and Mia was able to get through her first year.

Move to Maryland

Spring 2009

Dear Mistress Ali,

In February, after not having any communication with his sons since the night of the gun incident over a year prior, and very limited communication with his daughters, Dan called and spoke to the children and asked them to meet him for dinner. Not one of the children wanted to go. I talked to them and told them, "Just maybe your dad wants to apologize, so you should meet him." They all still refused to go. I then told each child that the other three were going and so I got them to go and meet with their dad. It was not very long before I regretted that decision.

Three of the four children came back to my home to inform me that their dad wanted to meet with them to tell them that he was moving to Washington, DC, for a new job.

121

They expressed to me that all their dad wanted was to tell them that he was leaving them to go to live with his mistress.

It was a horrible night. Kyle was emotional and crying from hurt and disappointment. Mia kept saying, "Let him go. We will be better off with him gone." Nick was devastated, so he called his uncle, who has been like a father to him his whole life. He had to vent about what his dad just told them. Dan did not give the children any information. He gave them a new phone number and that was it. He did not tell them the name of the company where he would be working. He did not give them an address where he would be living. He did not give them any information other than his new cell phone number.

The children were all devastated. I had a hard time dealing with their pain as it was a combination of hurt and anger. My oldest daughter went home to her husband and daughter, but called me on the phone to express her sadness. She felt such a loss that her dad, whom she loved dearly, would choose a mistress over his big loving family and his granddaughter. It was quite a night trying to be strong for my children and trying my best to make the pain in my own heart go away.

About two years before this, while Dan was still living at home, I received a phone call for him. I wrote the message down on a piece of paper and gave it to him, but not before making a copy for myself. The person on the phone said that they were calling about a job opportunity that Dan had been recommended for by someone in the Atlanta area. I assumed that the recommendation had come from you. When Dan came in I gave him the message and asked him what it was about and he said he had no idea. Later that day I walked out into the garage and there was Dan on the phone. I stopped and looked at him, thinking he was talking to you; however, I soon discovered that it was the company in Reno who had called him earlier, the same company he claimed he knew nothing about. Of course he was lying and he knew very well that you were helping him to get another job other than the one in Atlanta.

The night of the dinner the children said that Dan was leaving Georgia to start his new job in the beginning of April. The week after Dan left Georgia to start his new job, I got the piece of paper with the message from two years ago that I had filed away. I Googled the name of the company, but instead of putting Reno at the end of my search I put Maryland. The search results gave me a location and a phone number for the company in Maryland. I called the number and was directed to put in the first three letters of the last name of the person I was trying to reach. Upon doing that, I got a voicemail message from Dan, so I was sure that he was in fact living in Maryland with you. I had a work number, the name of the company, and an address for him. I had previously obtained the home address for your father where you were living when you moved out of Georgia. On a hunch I assumed that Dan was living with you in Maryland and probably in your father's house. I was right. It was clear why Dan did not give his children any information.

A man whom they had loved and respected was now leaving them, divorcing their mother, and going to live with his mistress in the home of and also with your eighty-year-old father and his wife. Who does that? Who lives with their married lover under the same roof with their elderly parents? Such disrespect. As if that was not hard enough for my children to accept and put behind them, you and Dan made it impossible for us to forget your name. You apparently were so insecure and in control of things that the phone number Dan gave to his children was attached to your phone plan. As a result, every time Dan called my home or the home of my eldest daughter your name was the name that showed up on the caller ID.

Unless someone walked in my shoes, they will probably never understand what it does to a person's psyche to keep seeing the name of the person who is part of the cause of all their pain. I begged Dan to please get his own phone or find a way to prevent your name from showing up on the caller ID. My grandchild and I would be watching TV and the phone would ring and whose name shows up on the television screen? Yours. This went on for months in spite of my begging Dan, cursing Dan, telling Dan to call his children on their cell phones since it wouldn't show up on there, but did he listen or care? No. I suppose you must have had knowledge of the expression "If he did it with you, he would do it to you," so you were monitoring his phone calls to make sure he was being faithful to you, I suppose. What a way to live.

Because Dan and I were still legally married and I knew how to access his account information, I continued to do so all while he lived in Maryland until the day our divorce became final. That certainly worked for me because it was on one of those calls soon after he moved that there was a transaction deposited into his account in the amount of $30,000. In doing my research I discovered that Dan had taken that money out of his 401K. That was the wrong thing to do for two reasons. First, since I spent all of my life with Dan, morally, whatever he had earned should have been for both of us, but he did not see it that way. I guess he had to bring something to the table in his relationship with you even though it meant taking from his children and wife. The second, and more important reason why this was wrong was, as you must know, having been divorced yourself several times, when someone files for divorce, the court automatically administers a restraining order on all the couple's assets. None of the parties should sell properties, cars, CDs, move money out of accounts or any investments, including 401Ks.

Of course Dan never imagined that I would find out what he did. I suppose that would have been his contribution to his new life with you in Maryland, I am guessing as a down payment on a home. Imagine he could do this while friends and family had to pay for his daughter's meal plans in school.

Now, while all of this is going on in my life, I have to admit I experienced a lot of emotional turmoil. This included periods of depression; however, because of the horrible person Dan was turning out to be, I had to become very vigilant, proactive, and aggressive to play his game! I could not have afforded to sit around crying all day or lying in bed being depressed. I had to fight for my survival and that of my children.

Throughout my life with Dan, he had been the breadwinner in the relationship and I had been a stay-at-home mom for most of our marriage. I had a couple of jobs off and on, but mostly part-time or evening shift as our children were the priority. Dan was also responsible for all finances, paying bills, filing our taxes, deciding when we made large purchases such as homes and cars. Dan had to have complete control over anything to do with our finances. Because of this power given to Dan in our relationship, I think Dan conjured images in his head of who I was and how capable or incapable I was of being independent and surviving. As a result Dan completely underestimated me throughout this whole fiasco and left me asking myself this question, "Does Dan know me at all?" The fact that he felt he would just take money out of his 401K and get away with it made me wonder if his brain cells were dormant. By taking money from his 401K after filing for divorce Dan was put in a position to be in contempt of court. Fortunately for me the court agreed.

When Dan moved out of Georgia to cohabitate with you in Maryland in March it became clear to me that this was a tragic turn of events for me and my children. I had no job, limited workplace experience, and no money. I knew then that I could not depend on Dan for anything. I knew then that my situation was only going to get worse. About one month before Dan left Georgia, my refrigerator stopped working. I called Dan, my daughter called Dan; we pleaded with him to help us and he refused. My son-in-law brought one for me that his friend was selling. I had no food in the house and no money, and because I still had my pride I did not share that information about my situation. I was ashamed and embarrassed to share that information with my friends and family. Then one day one of my ex-coworkers who had been laid off from the company I worked for was speaking with me and told me that she had just come from applying for food stamps. I made a decision then that I would rather expose myself and my situation to total strangers than to my family and friends, so I went and applied for food stamps.

That turned out to be one of the best things I did because not only was I able to have food in my home, but in the process of doing the application the employee processing it also asked me why I had not applied for unemployment benefits as I was entitled to it. My unemployment and food stamp benefits were both approved. That was a true blessing as I no longer had to be worried about my financial situation; though not the best, it could have been worse. I was now able to focus on my future as I knew that unemployment benefits were only for a short period of time. Once Dan began to live in Maryland his payment of the bills at my home became very sporadic except for the mortgage.

In the course of my marriage to Dan, I was responsible for the home and the children and he took care of the bills as the head of the household. My being a housewife worked well for us as we both felt and agreed that it was important for the children. After my last child entered nursery school at two and a half years old for four hours per day, I decided to go back to school. Dan did not agree as he felt that his job did not afford him any time to assume any responsibilities at home that he would have had to do once I began school. I attended school for one semester and did very well academically, but because of lack of cooperation from Dan and complaints from him that we could not afford it, I was unable to return.

During the course of our marriage, Dan never ever wanted me to work unless it was part-time or for a job with a flexible work schedule. Again, this was because he did not want to share household responsibilities if we both had full-time jobs and four children to raise. He always got his wish. So now Dan was advancing his career even though I was always there for him. He moved to Maryland with you, leaving me without a job or money and allowing my utilities to be disconnected whenever he felt like, while spending upward of $1,700 every month and living with you in Maryland with your dad and stepmother. All the while he continued to pay to have your grass cut at your home in Lilburn where your sister continued to live. This was absolutely unconscionable.

Here are the details of how much money Dan spent in four months of living with you in Washington, DC, from April to August. Dan spent $10,664.13.

APRIL

Date	Description	Amount
04-16	Withdrawal	$350.00
04-27	Withdrawal	$100.00
04-03	Giant Food Inc	$10.54
04-06	Withdrawal	$100.00
04-06	Crab Shanty Restaurant	$77.00
04-06	West Friendship	$30.51
04-06	Spirit Shop	$22.78
04-10	Ruby Tuesday	$67.00
04.13	ATM MD	$100.00
04-13	Giant Food Inc	$40.40
04-13	Vintage Cellars	$27.54
04-13	Bagel Bin	$13.09
04-20	West Friendship Cleaners	$59.77
04-20	Vintage Cellars	$36.02
04-20	Safeway Store	$26.19
04-20	Safeway Store	$21.90
04-20	Walmart	$5.89
04-22	Montgomery County	$40.00
04-22	Royal Farms	$30.00
04-27	Vintage Cellars	$25.43
04-27	Mc Donalds	$13.86
04-15	Chk Lawn Care (Lilburn)	$70.00
04-01	Lawn Care (Lilburn)	$45.00
04-28	K&G Baltimore	$74.20
04-28	K&G Baltimore	$642.30
04-29	Outback	$26.00

TOTAL=$2055.44

Eva-Marie

MAY
SAVINGS ACCOUNT

05-04	M\sfRess	$400.00

MAY
CHECKING ACCOUNT

05-04	Ft Mead Commiss	$163.49
05-04	Withdrawal	$100.00
05-04	Timbuktu Restaurant	$94.50
05-11	Giant Food Inc.	$91.47
05-11	Vintage Cellars	$42.38
05-11	Walmart	$16.96
05-13	Walmart	$128.20
05-13	Withdrawal	$100.00
05-14	Gwinnett H C5030	$333.64
05-15	Hilton Hotel	$107.11
05-18	Withdrawal	$200.00
05-18	Beyond Wir	$127.19
05-20	Mistress	$500.00
05-26	Mistress	$500.00
05-26	Sams Club	$242.95
05-26	Ft Meade Commiss	$221.41

WACHOVIA CHECKING

05-02	Withdrawal	$140.00
05-02	Café Nora	$24.00
05-04	Applebees Restaurant	$32.00
05-07	Ruby Tuesday Restaurant	$101.00
05-08	Indy 500 Restaurant	$21.40
05-15	Royal Packaging	$18.00
05-16	Royal Packaging	$22.25
05-23	Café Nora	$14.82
05-22	Vintage Cellars	$25.43
05-21	Chilis Restaurant	$30.00
05-22	Ruby Tuesday Restaurant	$38.00
05-23	Ft Meade Commiss	$62.48
05-29	Safeway Store	$20.14
05-29	Spirit Shop	$87.95
05-29	Crab Shanty Restaurant	$160.00
05-28	Withdrawal	$100.00
05-30	Sweet A Bakery	$16.09
05-31	Bagel Bin	$13.09

TOTAL=$4,295.95

JUNE

CHECKING ACCOUNT

06-01	Ruby Tuesday Restaurant	$375.00
06-01	Safeway Store	$15.15
06-08	MC DLC	$20.03
06-12		$500.00
06-15	Double T Diner	$22.69
06-22	Sams Club	$174.87
06-22	MC DLC	$67.97

WACHOVIA CHECKING

06-05	Mc Donalds	$5.29
06-05	Outback Restaurant	$90.00
06-08	Port of Subs	$8.57
06-07	Bagel Bin	$14.36
06-12	Travelers Gifts	$36.48
06-12	N.W Duty Free Liquor	$76.24
06-13	Ft Meade Commiss	$276.14
06-15	The Devons Grill	$20.00
06-16	The Devons Grill	$23.00
06-17	The Devons Grill	$52.00
06-23	Giant Food Inc	$15.55

TOTAL=$1,793.34

AUGUST

SAVINGS ACCOUNT

08-04	Debit	$100.00
08-18	Debit	$100.00
08-24	Debit	$200.00
08-31	ATM	$100.00

CHECKING ACCOUNT

08-03	Sams	$271.59
08-03	Vintage Cellars	$41.31
08-03	Double T Diner	$33.00
08-03	Walmart	$30.46
08-04	Giant Food Inc	$60.75
08-10	Debit	$100.00
08-10	CNF	$225.10
08-10	MC DLC	$39.85
08-11	ATM	$100.00
08-17	Publix	$17.63
08-17	Marriott Hiltonhead	$23.54
08-20	Clarks Outlet	$90.95
08-21	Giant Food Inc	$32.01
08-24		$166.06
08-24	Withdrawal	$100.00
08-24	Giant Food Inc	$33.30
08-25	CHK #733	$500.00
08-28	MCDLC	$44.40
08-31		$6.90
08-31		$6.50
08-31		$12.07
08-31	Majestic Deli	$34.68
08-31	Park Café	$49.40

TOTAL=$2,519.40

TOTALS

APRIL	$2055.44
MAY	$4295.95
JUNE	$1793.34
AUGUST	$2519.40

TOTAL=$10,664.13

While he was spending money on you and your family, my family and friends were taking care of his family. (I have replaced your legal name with the word "Mistress.")

In June, as Father's Day came around, my children were apparently overcome with sadness at the loss of their dad, not by death, but by desertion. About one week after Father's Day, my younger son, Kyle, informed me that he had found out where his dad was living. He decided to call the home instead of the cell phone number that Dan had given to them since he said his dad rarely answers his phone anyway. He told me that on Father's Day he called the number and asked for Dan and was told that he was not there. He said that the person he spoke to was your dad. Kyle said he was so sad at that time that he said to your dad, "This is Dan's son. Did you know that Dan has a wife and four children that he left while you are letting him live in your house with your daughter, who is his mistress?" My son said that the only response he got from your father was that both you and Dan are grown and he is not responsible for what you and Dan did. I felt very sad when Kyle shared this with me after the fact. First, he wasted his time researching information about where his father was living. Second, he called his father on Father's Day and was not able to reach him, especially in light of the situation at the time. And last but not least, I think my son was crushed at your father's response.

I do not blame your dad for what he said, but it had a very devastating effect on my son for some reason. I don't know if he expected sympathy from your dad, but after listening to him, I did not have the heart to tell him that he should not have called there in the first place. If his dad never gave him that number, clearly he never intended for him to have it. It appears that on that same day that my son was trying to reach his dad, Mia also tried to reach him and was unsuccessful. I later found the following letter in her room that she apparently typed and sent to her dad in the mail. She told me she sent a letter to her dad on Father's Day and he never even mentioned the letter, showed concern for her feelings, or demonstrated even one sign that he cared about what she said or how she felt. This is the letter:

I miss the idea of the father I should have had. I am grateful for everything you buy for me, but what I would appreciate much more are the things you cannot buy. Peace. Love. Happiness. I've grown up to know that my words, emotions, and actions don't have any effect on you, but stranger things have happened. "Who knows, lightening could strike." I don't dream of a perfect father, simply of one who loves his children eternally and unconditionally because they are his biological manifestations. They are half of him and half of the woman he chose, long before their creation, to love and live with "til death do [them] part." A father whose words and actions emulate this unconditional love. A father who is supportive and caring.

Today should be the day we celebrate you, honor you and everything you've done for us. Reciprocate the love you've given to us, yet the reciprocated actions you deserve shouldn't even be subjected to our worst enemies. Instead of a happy day, it's a day, for your children, that you have filled with regret and animosity. It's a day where the wounds from where you cut us so deeply are reopened so violently. A day we will forever spend in pain — whether we show it, and/or you acknowledge it, or not. But it's your day. I can only hope you use this day as a day of reflection and decide if as

a father, this is how you want to live the
remainder of your life on this earth and the
final Relationships you want with your children.
We're hurting and only you can properly
heal these wounds. Yes, you fathered four
children, but today is for fathers and you
no longer deserve it. It takes a man to be a
father. A father teaches his sons to be men.
A father sets an example for whom his
daughters should marry. A father loves

Returning to School

Dear Mistress Ali,

In August of that year, at fifty-five years of age and without a job, I decided to return to school and work on the degree that I had attempted to obtain on two separate occasions in the past. This decision was a very hard one for me to make, but the alternative was worse. I spoke to my family and my children and they were all very supportive. I had not been in a classroom in over fifteen years and I was not very computer literate. I knew how to send an e-mail and Google information, but aside from that my knowledge was limited. I was petrified at the thought and extremely intimidated by the idea of what I was going to do. I have a very hard time accepting failure and defeat. I am a very driven person and I felt that I could accomplish anything that I put my mind to, but

137

that feeling is very different when you walk into a classroom at fifty-five years old, especially when this is not by choice, but by necessity.

I started with a community college as I thought that would be easier. I also took classes later in the day so it was not as intimidating as I originally thought it would be. There were other mature students in the classes. The class sizes also consisted of around twenty-five to thirty-five students. Once I began classes, I felt pretty good and the experience was made even easier because I was an excellent student. The teachers liked me and respected me. Pretty soon, when the younger students realized that I got excellent grades, they not only respected me, but also wanted to befriend me. They always wanted to be in my group whenever there was a group project.

I must admit the first time I had to write a paper as one of my class assignments I was completely lost and had no clue what was expected of me. When the teacher said to the class that the paper had to be written in APA format I felt like the teacher was speaking another language. Determined not to fail, I commissioned one of my young nieces who had recently graduated to help me. I gave her the information that was given to me and she was patient enough to help me research the topic of the assignment. She gave me a former assignment of hers in the format the teacher requested us to use as a guideline for my paper. With her help and guidance, I received 96 out of 100 on my paper. After receiving that grade I felt a lot better as I now had an idea of how to produce quality papers. For the remainder of that semester and the following semester I did fine and enjoyed the experience of being in school as it took my mind off of the drama in my home.

Around this same time Dan began with his random bill payments again. In my last semester at that school, beginning in October, Dan stopped paying the Georgia power bill. I called him, his son called him, his daughter called him, and I pleaded with him, but all our efforts were in vain. By December I received a disconnection notice. I told Dan, and he told me he had no money. My week of final exams were about to begin, so I called my sister and asked her for the four hundred dollars to pay my bill to avoid disconnection. She promptly made a transfer to my account and I then paid the bill. The very next day Dan called and asked me if the bill was paid. I assumed that maybe he had a change of heart and was going to help us. I informed him that my sister paid it and if he would like he can help me by giving me the money to repay my sister. He then repeated to me that he had no money.

Two days later and the day before my last two final exams I discovered how cruel Dan really was. I came home from class and the garage door would not open. I got out of my car and walked to the front door to let myself in. Once I opened the front door, the alarm began buzzing with the trouble signal. I turned the switch on to get some light to try and fix the problem with the alarm. To my surprise and confusion, I discovered that we had no power. I immediately got on my cell phone with the power company. The representative then informed me that I was not disconnected because of lack of payment as they had received my payment and it was being processed. I asked the woman to explain to me why I was disconnected. She informed me that the owner of the account called after the bill was paid, and since there was no longer a balance, asked to close the account. I was beyond devastation. I had no power, no money, and no way of opening a Georgia power account. For no reason, all of a sudden, Dan had shut down the account because it was in his name.

At this time I could not think clearly. I felt like I could just give up. I sat in my living room and cried for hours. By the time I was able to compose myself, it was dark outside. I put a few things together and went to my daughter's house to spend the night there. Needless to say, I was in no condition or frame of mind to go to school the next day. I missed my last two final exams, resulting in two C's as my final grades despite the A's I had going into the exam. At the time I did not care about that. I was concerned about the food in my freezer and refrigerator that would spoil if I did not get power back. I was concerned about the rage and anger my son got into once he realized what his dad had done to us. I was concerned about finding a way to conquer the problem at hand.

I suddenly thought of putting a stop payment on the check and going to Georgia power and opening my own account. When I got to Georgia Power, armed with my ID and my checkbook, I approached the customer service agent and she informed me that I needed a deposit among other things that I just could not afford. I felt hopeless because I wasn't sure if there was anything I could do. I was frustrated and angry at the situation that Dan was putting me in. And lastly, I was desperate to get my life in order by whatever means necessary. I was so overwhelmed that I lost all control of my emotions and broke down in front of the representative. I confessed through my tears that my husband ran off to Maryland with his mistress and wouldn't pay the bills and I was in the home with no job or money and no power. She quickly became extremely compassionate and sympathetic and said to me in a kinder tone, "Don't worry, I will help you. What goes around comes around and your husband will get his." We determined how much I could afford to pay and she opened an account for me in my name. Later that day, even though the representative told me that she didn't think I would be connected until the following day, the power company came out to my house and once again I had power. One more challenge had been overcome.

In December, January, and February we continuously received bills from the gas company that were not being paid. Dan had access to all the bills online, so he knew that the balance for each month was being carried over from the previous month. Apparently, the gas company was not quick to disconnect their customers when the weather was cold so that their customers could have heat. Well, as soon as March came around we received a disconnection notice. I called Dan and again we repeated the begging and the pleading and he continued his lies about not having any money. By the end of March, the gas company disconnected our service. We had no heat, no money, no hot water, and again no ability to pay all of these bills. Every day for three weeks Kyle and I either had to go to my daughter's house to shower or we boiled water on our electric stove and filled buckets in order to bathe. This was stressful and painful as I continued to ask myself, "What could my children and I have done to Dan in our life together that he could be this wicked and cruel to us?" The worst part is I never got an answer to this day, even when the question was asked to him directly.

Once the gas was disconnected, I called the gas company and was very fortunate to speak to a representative who was willing to help me. The representative told me she would be able to help me if I had an address and phone number for Dan in Maryland. I gave it to her and she opened an account for me. The bill for the past five months, which was now over $1,000, was forwarded to Dan. I felt truly happy and blessed because the power and the gas accounts were now in my name. Now I controlled my own bills and payments. My services were restored and I had money in my account from the check I stopped to the power company. The best part of all was that Dan was still liable to pay both bills.

In spite of my receiving two C's on two of my courses, I graduated from the junior college in December 2010 *magna cum laude*. I was also accepted at Georgia State University in January with the scholarship that I received while I was in the junior college.

Kyle

Dear Mistress Ali,

Dan's focus seemed to have been on punishing me for not accepting his infidelity. Meanwhile, his actions of revenge impacted his children in ways that he will never understand, and have left permanent scars. Regardless of what Dan may think, feel, or say, the fact is these are still our children and I am, and will always be, the mother of his children.

Kyle was affected in so many ways by this drama, not unlike the other children. Although, unlike the other three children, he was privy to all of the cruel and wicked actions of Dan firsthand because he lived with me. Whatever was done to me in the home, including the disconnecting utilities, also affected our son.

In the spring of 2006, after being out of high school for a few years, Kyle made a decision to go to college as he knew that was expected of him. Dan and I gave him no choice, he either had to be enrolled in college or get his own apartment. He decided on college, so he applied and was accepted into a college in Macon, Georgia. Kyle had a neighborhood friend who was attending that same school and lived in his own apartment in Macon. All wheels were in motion for Kyle to begin school in August 2006 and I was very happy and proud of him for making positive steps toward a brighter future. He had plans to play football for the school, so he had made several trips to Macon in the preceding months. I personally had faxed several documents to the school for him, sometimes while he was at the school. Everything seemed to be going great for him; his plans were to be roommates with his friend James from our neighborhood until James graduated the following year. Kyle had begun to pack his stuff and do some shopping for his move to college for the first time, at age twenty-two, and he was happy, excited, and looking forward to his new life as a college student.

Well, three weeks before Kyle was to start school Dan moved out of our home and into your house in Lilburn. With all that was going on at that time and the way Dan acted like he did not care about anyone other than you, Kyle became quite torn about his decision to leave home and leave his baby sister and his mother by themselves to deal with what he considered a family crisis. He did not see the situation as a "mom and dad problem," especially since Dan had brought them into his immoral life months before I was even aware that you existed. I tried, unsuccessfully, to encourage Kyle to continue with this plans of going away to school, but Kyle, who happens to be my most sensitive child, refused to go.

I was heartbroken by his decision and in my heart hated you and Dan for all the many ways you both were changing my children's lives. I was too consumed with my own pain at that time to be more forceful with Kyle as I would have been under normal circumstances. The decision was made by Kyle and his decision was final. In retrospect, it seems that on that faithful day in August Dan left his family and my twenty-two-year-old son stepped up and replaced him as the new man of the house. Together with his older brother, Nick, and my son-in-law, they became the new father figures for Mia.

Apart from Kyle's career path derailing, his personality also underwent a complete change. My sweet, funny, sensitive, and caring son became constantly angry, argumentative, almost belligerent, and very hateful. I had no clue how to deal with those changes and I did not have anywhere to turn to get help for him. None of my family members could comprehend what I was speaking about since none of them lived in my home or even in the same state. His siblings were his greatest targets, after Dan, then me. I reached out to a professional for advice and they recommended that Kyle begin some therapy. Kyle was over eighteen and I could not make him go even though I felt that he desperately needed it. I tried talking to him about it; he refused. I pleaded with him; he refused. I had his siblings make subtle suggestions; that did not work.

When I tried to mediate and rectify any situation between Kyle and any of his siblings, I tried telling them what he was going through. They were far from sympathetic as they felt they were all going through the same thing and I was just making excuses for Kyle's bad behavior. I had no energy left to try and explain to them why Kyle had stronger, deeper, angrier feelings toward Dan and you than they did.

For example, before the fiasco with the power bill, Kyle called Dan twenty-two times in one day and Dan never answered his phone. Kyle then called your number. He never told me what he told you, but within two minutes of his call to you Dan returned his call. What do you think my son would feel when things happen like that?

Dan was speaking negatively about me the night he took them to dinner before he left for Maryland, but Kyle stopped him and told him not to speak about his mother.

Dan said to Kyle, "You have the keys to your car; you know what to do if you don't want to hear what I have to say."

Kyle then got up, said goodbye to Dan, and left the restaurant. Kyle came home that night and he was very upset and emotional about that incident.

From that night until this day, Kyle has never called Dan "Dad," but instead calls him Dan. When I asked him why he calls his father Dan, he said that Dan is no father. He, along with the rest of the world, believes that a father would never treat his children the way Dan was treating them. He said until Dan acknowledges what he has done to every family member and takes ownership of the destruction he has created, he will never call him dad.

Once Kyle changed his plans to attend college he began working and helping with the bills. When I lost my job, he paid some of the bills and I paid some with my unemployment checks. When my unemployment ended and I was in school with no job, Kyle paid all the bills by getting another job. It seems like the more he worked, the more he hated you and Dan because while we were struggling to make ends meet you were posting pictures of you and Dan on Facebook from your trip to New Orleans and your fiftieth birthday party. You also wrote about your trip to Vegas and your several trips to attend conferences for your AKA sorority.

These are all things that upset Kyle. He felt that the only concern that Dan had in life was you, and Kyle felt cheated and angry. In December 2010, Kyle was in a car accident around 4:00 a.m. At 6:00 a.m., I began to call Dan to let him know about his son. I called him around six times between 6:00 a.m. and 8:00 a.m. My calls all went unanswered. I was upset, furious, and extremely angry by 8:00 a.m. I called your phone number and you answered. I demanded, "Tell Dan to answer his f——ing phone! His son was in an accident." He promptly called me within a minute of my call to you. That is how irresponsible Dan became: a man who left his four children and grandchild in another state just to live with his mistress, and wouldn't even answer his phone.

I made a promise to myself that morning: I would not be calling him about anything again, because if his children were not important to him then nothing else was. That had been his behavior all during the period while he was still living in our home. As a matter of fact, that was why my children called your phone. Once Dan was not answering his phone we all knew that you were in his presence. So very pathetic.

To this day Kyle has not recovered from this breakup of his family. He speaks as if he hates his father, and absolutely despises you and your sister for calling our home and cursing him and his mother for no reason. At some point I was able to get Kyle to speak with a therapist. I think he could have been helped had he gone for a period of time, but he refused to go. I did, however, see a slight improvement in his attitude until January 2011.

Harassment

January 2011
Dear Mistress Ali,

For some reason, which I still do not understand, I began to get phone calls on my home phone from creditors for members of your family. First it was for your niece, then your sister, then your daughter. I called Dan and spoke to him about it. This was very, very upsetting to Kyle and me because it appeared that we were not able to forget about you and move on with our lives. I called Dan several times and asked him to take care of the situation.

One day my phone rang and when I answered the person requested, "May I speak with Ali?"

I replied, "Excuse Me?"

The person regretted this with, "I'm sorry," and hung up the phone. I immediately called Dan and told him what took place.

His way to deal with it was to say to me, "Ali is a common name. Why do you feel that call is connected to me?"

I was furious. I checked the number and the call was from Neiman Marcus. I again called Dan and gave him the number. I asked him to please take care of it so no one calls my home again. For some reason, Dan did nothing about the situation. I continued to be harassed by different creditors calling my home for your sister relentlessly. When the call came for your daughter, I sent you an e-mail out of frustration.

↩ Reply | ↩ Reply All | ↪ Forward | ✕ Delete | 📁 Put in Folder ▾ | 🖨 Print View | 👤 Save Address

From:
To:
Date: Mon, 7 Mar 2011, 19:49:41 -0500
Subject: FW:

I HAVE HAD ENOUGH!!!!!!!!!!! YOU BROKE UP MY MARRIAGE, YOU HAVE DESTROYED THE RELATIONSHIP DAN HAD WITH HIS CHILDREN AND EVERYONE HE HAS KNOWN FOR HIS 59 YEARS ON THIS EARTH. I HAVE NOT BOTHERED YOU OR YOUR FAMILY AND I HAD GOOD REASON TO. COULD YOU PLEASE TELL ME WHY YOU PEOPLE CONTINUE TO HARASS ME?????????? COULD YOU TELL ME WHY YOUR SISTER HAS USED MY TELELPHONE NUMBER FOR HER GLOBAL CREDIT ACCOUNT. IT IS MY PHONE NUMBER BUT YOUR LILBURN ADDRESS ACCORDING TO THE REPRESENTATIVE AT GLOBAL CREDIT. COULD YOU TELL ME WHY SOMEONE FROM NEIMAN MARCUS IS CALLING MY NUMBER ASKING FOR YOU?????????? I AM SOOOOO SICK OF YOU F...... PEOPLE. LEAVE ME AND MY FAMILY ALONE. YOU FOUGHT FOR DAN AND YOU GOT HIM WHAT THE HELL MORE DO YOU WANT?????????? YOUR CRAZY SISTER STARTED BY CALLING MY HOUSE TO CURSE MY SON AND MYSELF IN AN EFFORT TO FIGHT FOR DAN. NOW YOU HAVE HIM, REMOVE MY NUMBER FROM ALL YOU F...... PHONES. I TOOK DAN OUT OF THE GUTTER 35 YEARS AGO BUT HE FOUGHT HARD TO FIND HIS WAY BACK HOME. IF YOU PEOPLE CONTINUE TO DISRUPT MY LIFE AND HARASS ME I WILL TAKE THE

NECESSARY LEGAL ACTION.........LEAVE ME ALONE. THIS IS THE
CALM BEFORE THE STORM. ENJOY THE CALM WHILE IT LASTS.

DAN'S WIFE(THAT YOU CLAIM YOU DID NOT KNOW HE HAD. LOL)

🖾 | 🖾 | 🖾   ⬆ | ⬇ | ✕ | 🖾 Inbox

I also called you and gave you the information for your daughter. The next time I got a call, I called Dan and his solution was
that I should change my phone number. I told him he had to be
insane. I had had that phone number for over twenty years and I
had no intention of changing it because of his mistress and her
family. I would give the creditors his number and your number at
work and your cell.

One day I had had enough and I dialed your father's number
to ask him to ask his daughter and granddaughter to take care of
their delinquent accounts or call the creditors and have them
remove my number from their files. When I called your dad's
number, the phone was answered by a female. I identified myself
and before I could say another word, I received an onslaught of
profanity. I quickly realized that it was your sister, so all I said to
her in a calm tone was, "Ma'am, I need for you to pay your bills."

She cursed me and said a lot of very filthy things about Dan.
She also screamed, "Your husband is living in my father's
basement."

Apparently she was not happy with Dan, and for some reason
she thought I cared. She continued to reveal, "Dan has f— —
everyone in this house."

I responded calmly, "I am glad that all of you have had him,
but I need for you to pay your bills."

She continued to curse me and curse Dan at the same time. I assumed at that point that Dan was not one of her favorite people, but my attitude was one of amusement because she was so angry and hateful. The truth is that I understood your sister's anger at Dan. I would be angry too if my sister's married sixty-year-old lover moved into my parents' home. That is disrespectful and totally immoral. I would think that the least you and Dan could have done was get your own place instead of imposing on your eighty-year-old father and his wife.

This is one of the reasons my children have such little respect for Dan. Dan taught his children about respecting his home. They knew that there was no way in this lifetime that any of them could have a girlfriend or boyfriend sleep at our home. Yet here was the man who raised them and imparted these values doing the exact thing that he would not allow them to do and doing it in another man's home. Dan was taught by you how to treat and disrespect your father; clearly your sister did not agree and was rather furious. It was also quite obvious that she hated Dan at this point. This was the same person who helped you fight for him when she called my home and cursed my son and me because I was Dan's wife and I discovered where he was living.

After that phone call to your sister, I called my brother and told him what transpired because your sister made me uncomfortable with her threats to me all because I asked her to pay her bills and stop her creditors from calling my home and harassing me. My brother called Dan several times, but Dan, as usual, refused to answer his phone. My brother left messages for Dan to call him, but her never did. The next day my brother called me for your number. My brother called you and made it clear to you that one way or another those calls to my home had to stop or he would have to take some action. Soon after my brother spoke to you, Dan called him and he reiterated to Dan what he had told you. Dan promptly called the house and spoke to my daughter and got all the numbers for the creditors that I had given to both you and Dan previously. I never got another call again after that day. It just goes to show that Dan knew how to solve the problem he created, he just chose not to do so until my brother threatened to come to Maryland and embarrass you at work. Then all of a sudden the problem that we were begging Dan to fix for months was resolved.

In spite of who you were and all the trouble you and your family were creating for me and my children, my brother was never disrespectful or aggressive with you in any way. My brother never cursed you as your sister had cursed my children and me. He did threaten to come to your workplace and he meant it, but fortunately you and Dan took care of the problem so that it did not become necessary for him to pay you a visit. Around this same time your sister began to harass me and my family again by calling my home and hanging up the phone every time I answered. Even though your sister never spoke I knew that those phone calls were coming from someone connected to you.

I called my telephone provider and they were unable to help me. I called the police and made a report, but they were unable to do anything about it. The calls usually began around 11:45 p.m. and would continue until 1:00 a.m. Eventually I decided that every time I got a call at that time that disturbed my sleep I would call Dan and disturb his sleep. Well, I only had to call Dan on two occasions and then the calls stopped. That was my evidence that I was right all along and it was your sister or someone connected to you that was making those harassing phone calls to us. What did I ever do to you or your family that you all set out to harass me, even when Dan was no longer living in my home and was living with you in your father's basement?

My daughter called your father's house and asked for her dad because as usual he wasn't answering his cell phone. Your sister cursed my daughter using the most foul and profane language. When my daughter told me what happened, I immediately called Dan to let him know what your sister did to his child. Dan's only response was, "Simone had no right to call these people's house." I could not believe that he felt that was an appropriate response. His daughter was crushed and hurt at the lack of concern he showed for her and her siblings about the situation he got us into.

Once Dan took care of the harassing phone calls that I had been receiving, he proceeded to send me a very vindictive e-mail. Because you two were now both married and you were no longer just his mistress, I decided to copy you in the e-mail I sent to him. I also copied my brother so Dan could be made aware that I was no longer going to be in this alone. I wanted him to know that I had a family that would not tolerate what I was being put through any longer by him or you. I should have involved them sooner. The following is the e-mail you decided to write to me since I included you. I would like to respond to your claims:

Reply | Reply All | Forward | ✕ Delete | Put in Folder ▾ | Print View | Save Address

Subject: RE:
From:
Date: Fri, 23 Sep 2011, 19:05:11 -0400
To:

Please stop including me in your email messages. Please refrain from calling my office, my cell and my 80 year old father.

I cannot speak for _____, but I have never once called you, your siblings, your children, or cursed you, and threatened you. But you, your siblings, and all of your children with the exception of _____, have call me, my father, my job and cursed me, threatened me. I have always turned the other cheek. I am sorry that you and your family hate me, I don't feel that way towards any of you. It would have been nice if this could have ended civilly as consenting adults but it is clear that there is a permanent rift. I find that very sad. I wish you and your family well.
Please live in peace and have a happy and prosperous life. Try to let go of your anger, it is not good for your health.

Don't worry, I will not write again.

Sent from my iPhone

◄ | ▽ | ✕ | Inbox

1) As long as you and your family leave me and my family alone, there would be no need whatsoever to contact you or anyone else. Were you not aware of this at the time that you moved your married lover—my then husband—into your father's home? You knew that your father was eighty years old. My children and I had every right to call there for Dan. You two put your eighty-year-old father in that position, not us.

2) As of September 2011, you are correct; you have never called me, my siblings, or my children and cursed or threatened me. It was not necessary once you allowed your sister to do it for you. She called my home, my job, cursed my children and me with the exception of Mia.

3) You are lying when you say that all my siblings called you. I have six siblings and one of my brothers called you. He never cursed you. He did threaten to come to your workplace, yet that was only if your family did not put a stop to all those creditors calling my home looking for them or if your sister cursed me or any of my children again. Most would say that is within valid reasoning.

4) It is a complete fabrication when you say that my children cursed and threatened you. You are either a liar like Dan, or you are completely delusional, also like Dan. My children called your number many, many times as I have stated earlier. Whenever Dan was with you, he wouldn't answer his phone. Whenever they could not reach him, they would call you to tell their father to answer his phone. They were never friendly toward you and will never be, but they were never inappropriate either. My daughter Simone did call and curse your sister when your sister cursed me. I only found this out after the fact. I admonished her when I heard as I told her that it was unnecessary to go down to a level so beneath her. When your sister called *my home* and cursed both my son and me, neither one of us responded. When she hung up, I told Kyle to call his dad and let him know what your sister did. I never cursed you. I should have, but I never did. You even said that in your earlier letter to me.

5) You admitted that I didn't do anything to you. If I had been cursing you, why wouldn't you have mentioned that? The only thing I did was threaten you on several occasions to involve your supervisors and inform them about your relationship with my husband, your subordinate, in the workplace.

6) I did say in the e-mail that my children hate you. Could you please tell me what reason you could possibly have to hate us? When last I checked, I was the person married to Dan for thirty-six years. I am the one whose husband had an affair with you that led to divorce. I am the one whose life has been turned upside down, mentally, emotionally, physically, socially, and financially. My children have had their happy home and their lives as they knew it completely shattered, and now we must be appreciative simply because you don't hate us? I think you need a reality check.

7) I really think that you are delusional and your following statement is not even truly worthy of a response. "It would have been nice if this could have ended civilly as consenting adults." Let me remind you the only consenting adults were you and Dan. I never consented to have this nightmare. You find it "very sad" that there is a "permanent rift." This almost makes me want to question my own sanity, but I'm sure anyone, in my position or not, could tell you that I am not the crazy one.

8) Just FYI, I had a "happy and prosperous life" before you, together with Dan, decided to change that.

9) I am happy to say that I took your advice and got rid of my anger, writing these letters to you has been incredibly cathartic. It reminds me to cherish my health by doing what needs to be done for me.

10) I sincerely hope that you would take your own advice after reading my book and "Let go of any anger; it is not good for your health."

Simone & Nick

Dear Mistress Ali,

This drama has affected each of my adult children in a different way. Of all the four children, I think everyone, including myself, would agree that Simone was the child who was closest to her dad. We don't know if the fact that Dan's birthday is May 16 and Simone's is the day after had anything to do with it, but we always accepted the close relationship. We would joke that she understood Dan the most because of their birthdays. Simone loved her dad and he loved her to the point of spoiling her. When I said no to Simone about any situation and she wanted a different response, she would plead with her dad to talk to me and change my mind; sometimes he succeeded, and Simone would get her way.

When Simone was told by her siblings about her dad's affair, the stress and pain were immense. The hurt and disappointment caused Simone to begin to have health problems. Because I was not aware of the affair when my children found out, I had no idea what was causing Simone's health issues. Simone began to suffer crippling migraine headaches. She began to experience severe anxiety. She began to have problems with digestion. She was always tired and did not at all seem happy. I knew that Simone was deeply in love and happy with her new husband and he with her, so I had no idea what the problem was. Simone made several visits to the doctor and the only diagnosis that the doctor continued to give was that all of her physical problems were stress related. This was even more stressful for Simone, who was very close to me and felt the only right thing for her and her siblings to do was to keep the secret from me. In Simone's mind, keeping the secret from me would prevent me from experiencing any pain and heartache, but at the same time she was dealing with all of this on her own and not dealing with it very well.

Later when I found out about the affair, all of Simone's health issues went away except for the migraine headaches, which were completely linked to her dad. From that time to the present, 90 percent of the time when Simone has a migraine headache it's because she is in contact with Dan. Throughout Simone's first pregnancy, even though Simone and her husband were ecstatic at the news that they were expecting their first child, there was a dark cloud hovering over this joyful time for our family. This was because of what was going on between her mom and dad, whom she adored. Simone spent the majority of her pregnancy worried and upset. She worried about my health. She worried about her unborn baby. She worried about her dad. She worried about her marriage, all thanks to the two of you. Simone felt that her life was turned upside down and she had no control, which caused all her health issues.

You see, the problem is that Dan fabricated so many stories about our relationship that he actually believes his lies. If there were problems in our marriage before you, no one knew. Not me, not his children, not his family, not my family, and probably not even him. Dan was a good guy who did his best with what he knew. Like most marriages we had our ups and downs, but overall we had a good marriage. I caution my children to remember the dad that they grew up with and not to lose sight of the good man he had been all their lives. I petition them to not only see him as the person he had become as a direct result of the affair with you.

I can't imagine what Dan told you about our relationship, because any time I got Dan on his phone I always knew when you were present because of the hostility he exhibited. I would always say to him at those times, "Call me please when you don't have an audience." Then he would call me from work the next day. The children felt the same way; the only difference was he would be super nice and caring, and then they knew that you were in his presence. He is such a fraud.

Simone was again overcome with sadness and despair when she gave birth to her daughter. Although Dan was right here, living in my home and still working in Atlanta, he was not there for her in the hospital for the birth of his very first grandchild. After the baby was born, I called Dan several times at work before he came to the hospital to be with his daughter. I think Simone was completely crushed that her dad, whom she loved so much, was showing such a lack of concern and caring for her and her baby. He did go to the hospital eventually. Dan was becoming such a cruel person that no one recognized him.

A few weeks after the baby was born, Simone got into an argument with her dad about his behavior because she was totally frustrated. Dan did not like what she said to him. The next day Simone asked Mia to babysit for her and she agreed. Simone brought the baby over, and between Mia and me we took care of the baby. Dan did not look at the baby one time in the six hours that the baby was at the house. Even when we passed each other in the hallway while I was holding our precious grandchild, Dan was cold. He did not look at her, play with her, or even acknowledge her existence.

Later that day before Simone came to pick up her daughter, she called and spoke to Mia. The first thing she asked after saying that she was on her way was, "Did Dad hold or play with the baby while you were babysitting?"

Mia responded, "He hasn't even looked at her."

Think of what that did to my daughter. I was at a complete loss for words when Simone arrived to pick up her daughter; I could not imagine what would make a person do something so horrible to their daughter that they claimed to love. My sister was visiting that day and decided to confront Dan about his behavior. The explanation he gave my sister was that he was busy. Of course my sister demanded more. "Too busy to just look at the baby? Too busy to just smile at the baby?" He offered no further explanation or apology to his daughter or my sister. That was the monster we were living with.

Throughout the years of this drama, sometimes the children spoke to Dan, but most of the time they did not. During one of the periods of communication, Simone was expecting her second child. Dan was living with you in your father's house and Simone informed him that she was going to be admitted to the hospital to give birth on the twenty-ninth of June. She was scheduled for a caesarean section due to complications with the delivery of her firstborn. Two months before the birth, Simone was informed of this decision by her doctor and she immediately relayed the information to her dad. As the time drew nearer, she reminded him about the plan and expressed her apprehension about having to undergo the surgery.

When the time came, Simone was admitted to the hospital. Her husband, mother-in-law, and I were present; Dan was not. Everything went well and we now had a healthy baby boy as our new addition to the family. No one heard from Dan. Simone stayed in the hospital for a few days due to the C-section and still no one heard from Dan. Eventually, four days after the baby was born and shortly after mother and baby were at home, Dan called for the first time. This was despite the fact that he was told several times about the date of the delivery, the C-section, and all the necessary information. My daughter was again upset and tried not show it, but mentioned several times that her father does not care about anyone but himself.

Again, I lacked the words and wisdom to comfort my daughter about the situation or to make the pain that she felt go away. Our grandson was born on June 29 and Dan didn't come to see his daughter or even cared to see his grandson. When August came, you both drove to Georgia to register your car as your birthday was in August. I want you to think about this and tell me how my daughter should feel; her dad could not be there for her delivery, her dad could not make time to come and see his grandson, but every year, like clockwork, he came to Georgia in August so that you could register your car.

Sadly, once Dan abandoned his family and moved to be with you in Maryland, the only time he came to Georgia, besides for car registration, was when there was your sorority's convention in Atlanta. He has never come to Georgia to see his kids. When he comes to register your car, he never stays with his daughter. Basically, he sees his daughters for a maximum of three to four hours, depending on the day, no matter how many days he spends in Georgia. I hope this is shedding some light on the situation so you will have a better understanding as to why my children feel the way they do.

He never sees the boys because they do not speak to him. The reason they do not speak to him is because he denies taking out his gun on them in 2007 when he was arrested. He claims that one of the boys hit him, which never happened. The boys decided that until Dan takes ownership for taking out a gun on them and apologizes, they will never speak to him. Another reason they do not speak to him is because he lies about speaking to you in the car when Mia heard him. He also lies by telling anyone who would listen that I involved the children in the situation when in reality I was the last to know and Mia was the first.

Dan's behavior has lasting effects on Simone. Though she loves her husband very much and he loves her, Dan has deprived her of the feeling and sense of security with her husband. She feels that if her dad would do this to his wife of over thirty- five years and to his children whom he claimed to love, then no one is safe. I have tried as best as I could to reassure her that her husband is a good man and she needs to be happy without dwelling on the sad part of my life. I encourage her to focus on the happy years her family shared before you, Mistress Ali, became a household name in our lives.

Simone's relationship with Dan is very tumultuous and different, hence the reason for the migraines. Whenever Simone speaks to Dan, he relates things to her that he claimed I did or did not do, most of which are lies. Since Simone was an adult when the affair took place, she cannot be accepting of the lies that Dan tells and therefore it causes her a lot of grief. Dan continues to say that you pursued him, he did not pursue you. No one cares who pursued who, the fact is that he knew he was married and you also knew this. Dan lies to Simone about things that can be proved, which causes her to argue with him, the end result is her having a headache.

However, while Simone is filled with emotion over her dad and the end of her parents' marriage, resulting in negative effects on her health, Nick exhibits little to no response to the drama that has consumed our lives for so many years. Fortunately for Nick, the person he has been closest to his entire life was not his dad, but my brother, who also was one of Dan's best friends. Apart from being Nick's uncle, my brother is also his godfather and has a very close relationship with Nick. That is the person whom Nick has always turned to when discussing issues that come up in his life, like girlfriends and jobs. Nick has coped with this situation by talking to his uncle.

Nick has never showed any outward signs of rage, anger, pain, or sadness. The only time there was any sign of explicit emotion was with the gun incident, compounded by Dan's lies following the incident. Nick quietly took a stand to never speak to Dan again until there was ownership, some signs of remorse, and an apology. Well, he got two out of the three. I think he is still waiting for the signs of remorse, but realizing that it may never happen, decided to give Dan a chance after two of the three requirements were met. Unlike Kyle and Simone, who have been very conflicted with their emotions toward Dan, Nick has exhibited a constant pattern of indifference toward Dan. Nick has also made decisions based on what is most helpful and beneficial for his siblings and makes absolutely no decisions based on what is of importance to Dan.

Nick may go against his better judgment if I asked him. Sometimes I had to bring it to his attention that doing so would create something positive for his siblings as a group. He had no interest whatsoever in creating a better relationship with Dan. It is quite painful and emotional for all my children to hear Dan speak negatively about their mother. For whatever reason, Dan finds it necessary to speak about me constantly in a negative way when speaking to the children. This is not okay with them or with me. Dan lies about me every opportunity he gets. It does bother me sometimes, but most times it does not because the people like you whom he lies to I do not care about. The people who matter know that he is lying, so I am okay with that.

The sad thing is that when you are dating a married man who is living with his wife, you should expect lies, as no married man will tell his mistress that he is happily married and just wants to sleep with them. In this case, it backfired and that is why he hates me. Dan actually thinks and feels that he is the victim in this case. He is quite delusional and blames me for the demise of our marriage. I have no idea what planet he is from. He wanted his marriage and his family as he said a million times, but he also wanted his mistress. Well, in my world he is free to have one or the other but definitely not both, so now he has you.

His Friends

Dear Mistress Ali,

Unfortunately, Dan did not discriminate in inflicting his pain. Apart from myself and our children, Dan has caused great pain for the two close friends he had. He caused pain for his own family members, my family members, and all the people who love him most in the world. Dan made a decision to only have a relationship with people who would have a relationship with you, which consisted of a grand total of zero.

During the period of alienation from everyone, Dan's niece got married. This niece was very close to him. He did not attend the wedding because you were not invited. Dan's brother-in-law became ill and was ill for quite some time. Eventually, unfortunately, he passed away. Dan never

169

visited his brother-in-law and sister during the difficult period of the illness, nor was he there for his sister and her three children. Yet a few weeks after the funeral, the same person who abandoned his sister, nieces, and brother-in-law in their time of need, was "Walking for the Cure for our aunt and our cousin," as you stated in your Facebook post. What a fraud.

A couple of years prior to his brother-in-law's illness, when our daughter got married, Dan's brother-in-law and niece came to Georgia to attend the wedding. His brother-in-law was also Simone's godfather. His brother-in-law was a big help during that hectic weekend and we surely appreciated him. We loved him dearly and my children and I miss him a lot. Dan, however, barely speaks or keeps in touch with his sister and her children. That is so very sad because his sister and her family are caring, wonderful, loving people. My children and I love them deeply and they love us. They love Dan very much, but like everyone else, he does not seem to care about that. The question everyone seems to be asking is how a person can change so drastically.

Dan had loved his sister very much and had a very close relationship with her and her family. Dan has another sister who was his baby sister. Throughout our marriage, Dan treated her more like a daughter than a sister. He loved her, cared about her, loved her children and husband. A couple of years ago, her son graduated from high school and my children and I were invited to attend the graduation and the after party. Dan was invited and you were not. Because his sister told him that you were not invited, Dan called his sister on the phone, cursed her out, threatened her, and has not spoken to her again since then. It has now been two years since he has spoken to her.

Now, on the flip side of this, Dan has had a brother who lived in Florida throughout our years of marriage. They have never been extremely close. The children love their uncle a lot and I love him also. Dan always told me that they never got along, even when they were children. I just assumed it was sibling rivalry. The fact is that they never had a close relationship as brothers, even though his brother is a great guy. Well, since you became his mistress, he has reached out to his brother. He even took you to his home while he was still living with me, as I mentioned earlier. His brother welcomed you both in his home as his mistress where you both stayed on one of your weekend getaways. Well, his brother has now gained a brother and his mistress but lost his two nieces, two nephews, his great niece and nephew, and sister-in-law of over thirty years.

In our hearts we still love his brother, but the relationship has changed permanently. Dan's friend Ernest, the person who introduced Dan and me, has also been affected by Dan. Dan stopped communicating with his friend Ernest, even when Ernest's father became ill with a stroke and I informed Dan of the illness. Dan never called his friend, reached out to him, or even communicated with him until years later when Dan's brother (whom I only met twice in thirty-six years) passed away. Dan decided to go to the funeral and you accompanied him. Dan could not stay at any of his family members' homes, and for whatever reason apparently you both have a problem with hotels. So he then reached out to his friend and you both stayed as his guest for a few days. Ernest was also a friend of my family, years before he met Dan, and is my brother's best friend. He would never have been put in the position of accommodating you both if Dan had been up front and honest with him in the first place. Trust me when I say that will never happen again.

When Dan attended college, he met a young lady named Nadine and they became friends. Dan and I were engaged at the time. According to Nadine, Dan kept telling her, "I would like you to meet my fiancée, you two would get along." Eventually, one day we did meet and became fast friends. Her boyfriend at the time was also Dan's friend. Nadine and I were so alike that sometimes we joked about being sisters in another life. After Dan and I got married, the friendship continued. Nadine later got married to someone else and the four of us became very close. Years later, when we had Nick, our first baby, Dan wanted Nadine to be Nick's godmother. When Nadine had her two babies, I became the godmother to her beautiful daughter. The friendship between the four of us continued for years and I am still friends with them to this day. In the past, when we were all still friends, every time I would introduce Nadine to anyone I would tell them, "This is my friend Nadine." Dan would always interject and clarify, "*My* friend." The friendship Dan had with Nadine was a great one and there was a strong bond between them because Nadine loved and respected Dan a lot. When he began destroying our marriage, Nadine reached out to him in an attempt to help save our marriage.

Dan was crazy enough to plead to Nadine, "If you met Ali, you would really like her."

Nadine replied, "If I met her, I would kick her ass."

Dan has not spoken to Nadine since that day, years ago.

In May of my junior year, our friend Nadine was diagnosed with stage four ovarian cancer. Dan has never called her, not even once. My children, my family, all of Dan's family who knew Nadine love her and are praying for her, seemingly except Dan. We are all praying for her and she may have a miracle or she may not. If she does, my children and I would be eternally thankful, as we love her dearly. If she does not, it is God's will. Either way, the only thing Dan has done was send her a card eleven months after her diagnosis. The kind of person Dan has become is a mystery to me and everyone who knows him.

Growing up, my dad had a best friend whose daughter became one of my best friends in our adult life. Dan and I considered her family; her children are no different to me than my nieces and nephews. During our marriage, we lived in Trinidad for about seven years. During those seven years, her husband and Dan became friends. When Dan and I relocated to the United States, we returned to Trinidad several times. Whenever we returned to Trinidad, for whatever reason, we were graciously accommodated by my friend and her husband.

In June of my junior year, her husband was diagnosed with stage four esophageal cancer. In an attempt to get the best care possible, the couple traveled to Baltimore to Johns Hopkins Hospital. After a short stay at Johns Hopkins, he moved to Howard University's hospital in Washington, DC. My friend and her husband remained in Washington, DC for six months while he underwent treatment for the cancer. Dan was told by his daughter about our friend's diagnosis and prognosis. Sadly, he passed away while at Howard University Hospital. Dan never called, visited, or sent a card, flowers, or anything during their stay in Washington, DC. Our friend passed away in the month of September, and in February of the following year Dan finally sent a card to his wife.

My friend's husband's memorial was in Trinidad. Needless to say, Dan did not attend. Another sad part of this story is the daughter of this couple loved "Uncle Dan." While she was attending school in Canada, Dan and I celebrated our anniversary. She was another person who flew in to celebrate with us. Yet her dad is sick in a hospital in Washington, DC, for six months, passes away, and not one time did her "Uncle Dan" reach out to show some support even though he lives in Maryland. That was a difficult time for the whole family.

When Dan and I moved to Georgia years ago, I met this gentleman, George, who owned a transportation service. I was here with the children while Dan was in New York. Because I did not have a car at the time, I used the service quite frequently. George and I became friends, bonding over our Caribbean heritage and roots. He introduced me to his wife and we too became good friends. We were even pregnant around the same time. When Dan finally moved to join us in Georgia, I introduced him to my newfound friends. The husband and Dan became close and began to play tennis together every Tuesday night. The couple had three children: two boys and a daughter. The two sons became close friends with our own son, Kyle, and the daughter became close friends with our daughter Mia. That friendship began over twenty-three years ago and to this day my children and I consider them family. We love them dearly and they love us. We have a bond that will not be broken. Dan, on the other hand, has treated them the way he has treated everyone else. Once he left Georgia, he seemed to have ended his friendship with everyone.

George tried to keep the friendship. He would call him often. Dan, however, would always tell him he would call him back, but he rarely would. Dan would come to Georgia and never even called or visited him. This went on for a long time, but being the good friend that he is, George would continue calling Dan on occasion. Dan eventually would call him once in a while.

Two years ago, our last daughter graduated from college. Dan was at my home with my family and I invited George and his wife over. While he was at my home for the graduation dinner, Dan asked George if he could bring you over to their home to meet them. George, having good sense, told Dan that he did not think his wife, Sandy, was ready for that. The following day, Dan visited George at his home, where he proceeded to ask Sandy the same question. She told him in the sweetest, kindest way possible that that was not an option, that day or any other day. She told him how much she loved him but did not respect the fact that he ended his marriage by bringing someone else into his marriage. As usual, he tried to bring in some lies about me and why he wanted out of his marriage, but he was speaking to the wrong person. Sandy then told him that she did not care if I was a serial murderer. The right thing to do if he was that unhappy was to get a divorce and then start a new relationship, emphasizing it should not be the other way around. She truly loves Dan as a brother, and told him that, but held firm that he was never to bring you to their home, even though he will always be welcomed. Well, he did not like that, so I do not suppose he will be visiting her home again.

When I was pregnant with our third child, thirty years ago, Dan introduced me to a friend of his family named Jackie who was an OB/GYN. Dan wanted her to be my doctor during the pregnancy and I obliged. Throughout the course of my pregnancy, Jackie and I became friends. Dan's family had been friends with her since Dan was a baby because Jackie's brother- in-law and Dan's mother were cousins. Dan knew Jackie years before she became my doctor and we became close friends.

One month before Dan moved to Maryland to start his new job, I received the news about the death of Jackie's only child, who had passed away quite suddenly. I immediately informed Dan. Dan called Jackie that day, but she was in no condition to receive calls. He left a message with the person on the phone and asked them to let Jackie know that he called. That was five years ago.

Jackie has been living in Maryland over twenty-five years and Dan is very aware. We have visited Jackie in Maryland as a family when our children were much younger several times. Even though Dan lives about ten miles from Jackie in Maryland, since the death of her son, aside from that one phone call he made, he has never contacted Jackie again. He never attended the funeral, he never sent a card, flowers, or offered any condolences in any way to a person who had been in his life for sixty-two years. This is also the same person who delivered his third child and who has been nothing other than a great friend to him. How sad!

The reason for this behavior is, I assume, that Dan really cannot take you around anyone who is family, a friend, or really close to us as a couple. Because of his lies that he told you and because he knows that no one with morals will welcome you, he stays away completely. I would like you to keep track of all the relationships you two have destroyed and all the lives you two have affected while you are trying to create an impression to the world that your relationship was a match made in heaven. It is far from it.

Meditation & Divorce

Dear Mistress Ali,

After the divorce was filed in 2009, and prior to the final divorce decree in 2011, Dan and I were ordered by the court to attend mediation in an effort to settle our divorce without having to go to court. We had two sessions of mediation; neither of them went well. Throughout the proceedings I felt that the guy sitting across from me was a total stranger. He was mean, angry, uncaring, and showed no signs of remorse for the messy drama and pain that he had caused me and his children. If it were up to Dan, I had the feeling that he would not have cared if I were left penniless and living in a shelter with his youngest son and daughter.

179

Fortunately I had retained an attorney against Dan's request. Dan had asked for us to settle our divorce without an attorney because he knew I had no money and he claimed he did not have any money either. I may not have had money, but I still had sense. Even though I told him I could not have afforded an attorney, which was the truth, I did have one, thanks to the generosity of our friend Nadine. At the first mediation session, Dan was so angry that I had an attorney that he became entirely too combative with my attorney and the mediator. That session was a complete waste. I was very happy that I had an attorney because Dan could not be trusted and had no intentions of doing anything for me or giving me anything after thirty-six years of being together.

The other occasion of mediation was equally unsuccessful. At that point it was decided by the court that our divorce would have to go to trial before the judge. I was happy about that and had no doubt that I would be better off. Our divorce was scheduled for a Monday morning, March 21, 2011. My attorney requested to meet with me the previous Friday to go over the process with me and to discuss all the possible outcomes. From the day the divorce was filed in 2009 to the Friday before the divorce in 2011, Dan had never admitted to me, my lawyer, or even his lawyer, his affair with you. He claimed irreconcilable differences as the reason for the divorce. I claimed adultery. Fortunately for me, you joined Facebook and could not stop posting information about you and Dan and your life together before and after our separation, but all before our divorce. Even luckier, I saw and printed everything you posted.

During my meeting with my attorney on that Friday, he began telling me that our divorce proceedings may last longer than planned because he would first have to convince the court Dan committed adultery and is presently living with his mistress. I asked my attorney if having pictures and evidence would help. He asked me if I had pictures and when I said yes and produced the pictures you posted and all the posts you wrote about you and Dan, my attorney acted as though he had just won the lottery. He took the papers from me and faxed all the information to Dan's attorney before the close of business that Friday afternoon. I can only assume that Dan's attorney was not a happy person at that point, having a client who lied to her for the two years she spent preparing his case.

On Monday morning, when Dan arrived in court he looked as if the wind had been knocked out of his sail. For the first time since the drama began, Dan appeared humbled and deflated. I will never know what transpired between Dan and his attorney between Friday evening and Monday morning. I can only assume that it had not been good.

His attorney was late for court. She spoke to him harshly, and when our case was called, the judge offered an opportunity for mediation one more time at a cost of $150 an hour. I declined the offer. I was ready to go before the judge. Mediation had not worked when it was free; I saw no reason to seek a resolution through that same process but this time having to pay for it. Dan and his attorney, on the other hand, apparently did not want to have our case heard before a judge, so they chose mediation, for which Dan would assume all the cost. I agreed because I felt that I had nothing to lose and I felt at that time that two lawyers were working for me and Dan had none.

At the end of four hours of mediation, both parties and their attorneys, together with the mediator, came to discuss everything that was mentioned and agreed upon with each of us individually with our respective attorneys and the mediator.

Before the discussion began I asked if I could say something. I proceeded to say, "I do not know what the outcome of this is going to be, but I would like to make a request to the court. In the event that Dan and I remain joint owners of the marital property, I would like the document to be worded in such a way that if Dan should remarry—"

Before I could complete my request, Dan interjected. He said in an angry, hostile tone, "That would never happen."

I reminded him, "I never thought that I would be in court getting a divorce either, but we are here." I then proceeded to continue with my question to the court, "As I was saying, I would like to ask the court to have the document worded in such a way that if Dan should marry his mistress and he should pass away, that his mistress and I do not become joint owners of our marital home."

Before the attorneys or mediator could respond, Dan again said, "That would never happen."

Everyone ignored him at that point. The court did better than I had expected, as stated in the final divorce decree dated April 26, 2011. It said, "Defendant (me) shall retain sole control, interest, use, possession, and ownership of the marital residence of the parties to Wit: our address, for which Plaintiff (Dan) shall pay all mortgage payments in a timely manner as due and payable for the next seven (7) years through May of 2018." That is what I consider just.

Let the record show that Dan was married before the thirtieth of May 2011, less than one month after stating in court, when I suggested that possibility, that "that would never happen."

In the final divorce decree it stated that Dan should retrieve his tools from the marital residence on or before May 15, 2011. Dan returned to Georgia to register his vehicle the second week in May, came to the home to retrieve his tools, and visited with each of his children. On May 30, 2011 you posted pictures on Facebook of a Kappa Alpha Psi Columbia, MD Alumni Chapter's Annual Black and White Affair at Turf Valley, where you indicated you were married by the change in your last name. If there was any doubt, on June 4 you wrote a post with the words, "my husband and I."

This was the first time that my children became aware of their father's nuptials. Again, this was upsetting and devastating to them for several reasons. What was most painful was the fact that they saw their father two weeks prior, and he made no mention of his plans. He spoke to Nick on May 25th for his birthday and made no mention of his marriage. Three days later, they learn about it on social media from the mistress/wife. At that point the children made a decision that they were sick and tired of the rollercoaster relationship they had been having with their dad and decided to end it.

Dan called the children from time to time after that and apparently no one was answering their phone. He called me afterwards to inquire about the children and why they were not answering his calls. I said to him that the children were angry and hurt that he got married and neglected to have the common decency and respect to share that information with them. He was with them two weeks before you got married and yet neglected to say anything to them.

Dan's angry response was, "When I was in Georgia three weeks ago, I had no intentions of getting married."

He annoyed me with his angry response, so I said to him, "How could marriage be so sudden? I know the whore is too old to be pregnant, so pregnancy could not be the reason for the urgency. Did she hold a gun to your head?"

At that point Dan hung the phone up on me. I guess he did not want to hear what I had to say. The fact remains that was the end of the conversation between Dan and I, and needless to say, without my involvement and begging the children to please speak to their dad it was not going to happen!

In August of that same year, both of you again came to Georgia since it was your birthday month and you came to register your car. Our youngest daughter Mia always maintained communication with Dan because he occasionally assisted her financially, in addition to the fact that he was court ordered to continue to pay her car note. At times, when the children were speaking to Dan, they made it clear to him that they never want to meet you. He is not to mention your name in their company and they wish to have nothing to do with you. Dan was fully aware of this and he was obligated to comply with their wishes if he hoped for any relationship with them at all.

In August, when Dan came to Georgia he made a plan with Mia to meet him at a store in the neighborhood as she needed some items for school that Dan was going to purchase for her. Mia said that as soon as she parked her car in the parking lot she saw Dan walking into Walmart with a female. She assumed it was you and therefore refused to come out of her car. She then called her dad on the phone a couple times, but he did not answer his phone.

Mia was about to leave to return home when her dad called her back. "Where are you?"

She responded, "I am just leaving the parking lot to go back home because when I pulled into the parking lot I saw you walking into Walmart with that woman and I do not want to meet her."

"I do not know what you are talking about; I am alone," he insisted.

"Daddy, I saw both of you walking in."

"Mia, would you please park your car and come inside? I assure you I am alone."

"Okay, Daddy. I hope you are telling the truth, because if you are not, you will be very embarrassed when I come inside."

Mia did go in. As soon as she kissed her dad, he said to her, "The same person you don't want to meet was willing to cosign your loan for you though."

Mia did not respond but felt that you were with him, but must have been told to remain out of sight. We will never know, but we do know that Dan saying that you were willing to cosign a loan for Mia made the children all angry as this was Dan's way of trying to make the children feel guilty about never wanting to meet you. But guess what? They do not care.

The next day, Dan met with Mia for breakfast. Mia said that as soon as they placed their order Dan said to her, "Mia, now that you know I am married, you still do not want to meet that person?"

Mia said no.

Dan did not say anything else about the matter. Their meal came and they ate. That was the first time that his marriage came up with any of his children. Mia was the only one of his four children that he saw during that visit. He left to go back to Washington, DC, without even seeing his one-year-old grandson and four-year-old granddaughter. Dan thrives on playing the victim. He never saw his other children before he left either because he did not want to acknowledge the children's pain or hurt about finding out about his marriage on Facebook. His response to their feelings was to be more angry than they were and ignore them completely.

Bittersweet December

Dear Mistress Ali,

The year 2011 has ended. I begin 2012 with joy and optimism. My divorce is final, my mortgage will be paid, and you and your family are now a distant memory. There is peace in my home, and I am looking forward to beginning my senior year in the fall. Sadly, there is no communication between Dan and his children or grandchildren. All I can do is pray for him that one day he can be the dad he once was.

In the beginning of my senior year, another dear friend was diagnosed with brain cancer. Needless to say this was a very sad time for me. My friend with ovarian cancer lived one hour away from my home. I visited her often; I went with her on several occasions when she was scheduled for chemotherapy. I had to continue to be her friend in every way possible regardless of my own personal responsibilities. I did the best that I could to keep in touch with my friend whose husband was ill. Phone calls were the only means of support that I was in a position to give at that time.

Though happy to begin my senior year and excited to start my internship, there were these dark clouds hovering over my life. While I struggled to be there for my friends, they were all going through the most difficult challenges of their lives. I was fighting to maintain a positive demeanor. I struggled to maintain my grades, attend class regularly, and complete my assignments. Occasionally I had to miss class to be in Rome, Georgia, with my friend, of which my professors were very understanding.

Sadly, my other friend's husband passed away in September. I had no choice but to be excused from class to attend the funeral in October in Trinidad. In December, when my winter break began, I decided to go back to Trinidad to visit my friend to spend a few days with her.

While on my visit, all the way in Trinidad, on December 9th, 2012, you called my phone on more than one occasion. It was not until I returned to Georgia and turned on my phone that I saw your missed calls. There was no need to listen to your message at the time, because my oldest daughter had already called me and informed me that you had called her. Now remember my husband and I had been divorced for almost eight months and you were married for almost seven. All the harassment, intentional or unintentional, malicious or non-malicious, that I had been receiving from your sister, creditors, or anyone else connected to you had stopped after my brother intervened, so there was no need for you and I to ever communicate again. My children had never met you or ever had any communication with you other than to tell you to have their father call them. You can imagine my daughter's shock and bewilderment to answer the phone at 11:30 p.m. on December 9 to hear your voice on the other end.

As a mother myself and a person with compassion, I was saddened when my daughter called me in Trinidad to tell me that your daughter had been shot and killed. My heart went out to you because no parent ever wants to bury their child. Regardless of how much I despised you, I felt deep compassion and sympathy for you. It was not long before I became really angry with you. You want to know why? This is the conversation you had with my daughter less than twenty-four hours after your twenty-one-year-old daughter was shot and killed.

Conversation Transcript:

The recording picks up with you saying, "And it's no, no part of my fiber can possibly believe he was not good to you . . . guys. He was married to your mother for a long time and I know they raised you guys right. I know this with all my heart. So please, whatever's going on with you guys, don't worry about me. I'm okay. Hey, love your dad . . . so . . . ."

Simone sighs.

You continue, "I need you to love your dad. I need you to understand that you're not promised tomorrow. And he's not; he's sixty years old! He hurts . . . when nobody calls him to say, 'Happy birthday, Dad.' He was a good dad. And I don't want him to be sick, or not die . . . I don't wanna not be able to say that his children

189

cared enough about him. Don't worry, I'm okay. You don't have to like me, I don't want you to. You don't have to. It's not about me."

Simone says, "It . . . it isn't about you."

"You need to understand that you don't have a second chance to say I love you. It's not about me and I'm not trying to make this about me. I just want you to know. I want you and your dad to be okay. Because he loves you. And he doesn't . . . and he loves you . . . . no matter what you think. It's not about . . . you. He loves you with all his heart. All his heart, so please . . . you know, don't worry about me. Just please, make up. Whatever it is. Whatever it takes. You know, whatever it will take. I just want you to be all right with your dad. 'Cause . . . I can't describe to you. You're a mom. You can't . . . I can't describe to you how I feel, with my baby died. I mean dead, and I can't . . . I can't do anything. I'm powerless. So please take advantage of the time you have left. He's sixty . . . he may, I don't know, you know, we don't know how many more years we'll have. She was twenty-one. She *just* turned twenty-one, so she's a baby."

Simone attempted to sympathize, "Good gracious."

"So please, please, don't . . . don't take the time you have with a wonderful man for granted because he loves you. He loves you. He's never said . . . he's always talked with me about you and Mia and Kyle and Nick with especially about how great his children are. And it hurts him he can't share. So just . . . uhh . . . he doesn't know I'm calling. I'm up in the bathroom. I gotta go; he's coming now. I gotta go. Bye."

Simone tried to offer her condolences for your daughter but the call was already disconnected.

This is the reality; your daughter's remains were lying in a morgue in Georgia. You were in your home in Maryland and you were calling my phone repeatedly. Why? When you were unsuccessful in reaching me, you called my daughter. The entire conversation you had with her was about Dan. Again, I will reiterate what I said earlier in this book. Dan needed a woman like you. I could never have been the woman you are. Your only daughter was shot and killed, and less than twenty-four hours later you are discussing with my daughter, someone you do not know, all about your husband's pain, nonetheless. Your daughter could not get your undivided attention even in her death. How very sad. To this day I cannot imagine what you were calling me for; I am grateful I was not in the country at the time to receive your calls.

Well, prior to your daughter's untimely death, Dan had spoken to Mia and told her that he was coming to Georgia on December 14, 2012, to attend her graduation on Thursday, December 20, 2012. When they spoke, Dan also told her that he wanted to try and meet with his other children when he came. On Monday, December 10, he spoke with Mia again, telling her that he was coming two days earlier than planned as he had some business to take care of. How sad it is that at no point in that conversation, or several other conversations later, did he mention your daughter's passing.

Mia is the only child that has always kept in communication with Dan. I have always encouraged that, even when he frustrated her. Dan was obviously unaware of your conversation with Simone, and obviously did not consider your daughter important enough to even mention her to Mia. He was therefore unaware that we all knew.

On Thursday night, December 13, someone called my house asking to speak to Dan. I informed them, confused, "Dan does not live here anymore."

The person thanked me and I hung up the phone, but not before writing down the number as I found it was very odd since Dan had not lived at this address for five years. On Friday December 14, Dan called my house and proceeded to ask me to meet him somewhere for lunch as he wanted to speak to me. I declined the invitation because I did not want anything to do with him. I told him whatever he wants to speak to me about can be done on the phone. He then said, "I would prefer to have this conversation with you in person."

I informed him that I didn't care what he preferred. It would have to be on the phone or not at all. He agreed and proceeded to tell me that he would like my help because he wants to try and fix the relationship with him and his children. I didn't think twice about his request, because I always prayed that one day he would come to his senses and try and heal his children's hearts. Before we continued with any further conversation, I told him about the phone call I had received the night before and I gave him the number. As soon as I did that he got very angry and informed me who it was. It happened to be his old boss from the center where he worked in Atlanta, also your friend. I, too, got angry when he told me who it was, because she, of all people, knew very well that Dan did not live at my address. I could only conclude that she was monitoring his whereabouts so that she could keep you informed.

When I agreed to help Dan, I made it clear to him that I will only do so on one condition. It was that anything I asked him he would answer, and answer truthfully. I can usually tell when he is lying, but he agreed. I began the conversation by asking him when he arrived in Georgia. He informed me he came a few days ago. I asked what prompted his early arrival.

"I had to take care of some business." He dodged giving me an explicit answer.

"Did your wife come to Georgia also?"

Dan was dumbfounded (or just dumb). "Why? I don't understand the question."

"That requires a simple yes or no. You don't even have to answer, but then you could just find somebody else to help you with your children. I am going to hang up now."

Cornered, he begrudged, "Okay, okay, she is coming next Wednesday because we have some furniture in the house in Lilburn that we want to take back to Maryland. She is coming so she can ride with me in the U-Haul."

I offered, "Let me give you some advice. You want to begin to fix your children? Tell that whore to refrain from calling them, regardless of her reason."

He blindly and condescendingly defended, "She does not call the children."

I began, "Clearly you do not know what she does and doesn't do—"

"The only thing I am sure about is that she does not call the children," he insisted in an extremely hostile tone.

Frustrated, I yelled, "You know so goddamned much about what she does and doesn't do, yet you don't know she is calling me and your daughter to tell us about her daughter being killed?"

Dan was silent for a few moments before he said, "What are you talking about?"

By now I was infuriated, "Listen to this," I demanded and I played the recorded conversation from my daughter.

Dan was completely silent.

I explained, "If you want to fix your children, start by apologizing to your daughter for that woman having called her. *You* married her. She is *your* prize. Neither I nor the children wish to be involved with her or her family, nor do we care to know what happens in her family. Imagine you are now the stepfather to a child who lost her life in a gang-related shooting. Imagine you are the same father of two sons whom you never permitted to wear their caps backward because, according to you, 'only thugs and people who belonged to gangs wore their caps like that.' The boys never did."

There was no response from Dan

Now, I was curious. "When you got involved with that woman, did you know her family was so ghetto?"

"Of course not."

Well, that response tickled me, because I honestly did not even expect a response to that question. Because I was in control of the situation, Dan was forced to answer my questions and even volunteered information that I did not know or ask about. He told me how your sister did not like him. He explained how she created such drama at your dad's house because of her disrespecting him. He went on to divulge that your sister can never visit your home because of a restraining order that you have on her.

Something that I just cannot wrap my brain around or relate to is what Dan told me about your daughter's funeral arrangements. He let me know that he was the person who took care of your daughter's cremation and that you never even saw your daughter after she was murdered. I am trying my best not to judge you; maybe I am the odd one. There is no way that I can understand how your daughter was murdered on December 9 and you never made an appearance in Georgia until the nineteenth, after everything was done. You just drove down to drive back with the furniture and collect your only daughter's ashes. Unbelievable.

Dan also told me that no one in Maryland liked him because they were jealous of his relationship with you. I feel so sad for him because there were so many people in his life who simply adored him. As much as I feel sorry for him, he'd made his choices and now he has to live with them.

While Dan was here for the week prior to the graduation, I spent three days in a discussion with each of the children and with Dan. The kids absolutely refused to speak with him no matter how much he wanted to speak with them. I decided to speak to each child individually as I felt if I could convince one, I would have less difficulty with the next, and so on. They operate as a group, as I explained to Dan. Unless all four agreed to give him a chance, it could not work for him to talk to one or two and leave out the others. They felt it was all or nothing.

The first and easiest child to agree to communicate with him was Simone. The following day, Saturday, I was speaking with him on the phone about some of the feelings that the kids expressed. Simone called at that very moment to ask me to meet her for breakfast with her kids. I put Dan on hold to take the call and when I came back I informed him I had to hang up to go meet Simone and the kids for breakfast, he then expressed his desire to join us, but I explained I would have to ask Simone. Once I did, she said that he could come provided I got there first. I relayed the answer to him and he agreed to meet us there. I got there about twenty minutes before him so that I had the opportunity to have a conversation with Simone. I asked her to please give him a chance and to let him be a part of his grandchildren's lives.

Prior to hanging up the phone with Dan, I told him what to say to Simone as soon he saw her, which was to apologize for his wife calling her. I also suggested that he avoid offering an explanation about anything. I told him to avoid any conversations about his job, his life in Maryland, or his wife. I advised him to make his entire focus center on his children and grandchildren. I also pleaded with him to not get an attitude no matter what any of his children said to him, because their feelings are what they will want to express and he needs to listen. He needed to try and empathize; that is all the children wanted at this stage.

I have to admit that Dan took my advice and the breakfast went very well. The grandkids were not very receptive at first because they did not know him. My granddaughter was sitting right next to me and I kept telling her, "Tell Grandpa what you just told me," or "Show Grandpa what you just showed me on your mom's phone." I really tried hard and prayed quietly that everything would be okay. I even subjected myself to accepting a kiss on the forehead from Dan, all in an effort to make my grandkids feel at ease with a man they did not know. By the end of the breakfast my granddaughter was asking him which car was his and if she could ride with him to her mom's car. I left them all in the parking lot and went on home. Apparently when they left the parking lot Dan wanted to buy both the kids toys, so they all went to the mall, where he purchased each child a toy. My daughter, who was always very close to her dad, found it easy to reopen communication with him. She felt almost as if she had her dad back.

The next challenge was my oldest son Nick. Surprisingly, he was not such a challenge after all. Once he heard about how things went at breakfast he was much more open to giving Dan an opportunity to try and make amends. After the mall, Dan decided to visit with Simone at her home so he could spend some more time with the children. That worked for Nick because he did not want to meet with Dan anywhere by himself. Nick decided he was going to meet with him at Simone's house the following day, which was Sunday, and he did.

The biggest challenge I had left was Kyle. He is the child who lived with me and was subjected to all the cruel things that Dan did to me and indirectly did to Kyle. I asked Kyle to please speak to his dad as a favor to me, and promised him that I would never ask him to do anything like that again. My conversation with Kyle was quite exhausting because he wanted no part of Dan. He never forgave Dan for the gun incident; he never forgave him for having our utilities disconnected every time he felt like it. He never forgave him for basically abandoning his family. After a lot of debating, which inevitably included some shouting, there was a lot of rage and pain from Kyle and a lot of begging on my part. In the end, Kyle finally agreed to speak to his dad.

Dan came to the home that Sunday evening because Kyle refused to go out of his way to meet him anywhere else. I remained upstairs when he came, so I never saw him. I was so very proud of my son for the mature way in which he handled his father. There was absolutely no shouting, not even a slightly raised voice. Kyle got everything off of his mind and heart, and Dan listened. Dan was not the only one to benefit from the conversation because it also helped Kyle tremendously. For the first time in all the years of drama, he was able to confront and face his dad, releasing some of the rage and pain that he had been holding in.

The graduation took place a few days later without incident. I felt very sad for Dan. All of my family came from Miami and Canada for the occasion and it was sad to watch all these people who had always loved Dan like a brother disregard and ignore him, just as one would do to a perfect stranger.

As far as I was concerned, Dan got an A+ for the effort he made that week. He began to form a bond with his grandchildren, his children were all speaking to him, and he was as engaged and concerned as he used to be when he was a dad in the home. I was happy and relieved as I always wanted the best for my children. I think that having a relationship with their dad could only be positive.

My children took my daughter and I on a cruise following the graduation as a gift to Mia and a gift to me in anticipation of my graduation six months later. Before we left for the cruise, Dan was in contact with the kids. He bought them all Christmas presents. He took care of Mia, helping move her things for her apartment in South Carolina back to her home in Georgia. Dan helped Kyle with an issue with his car. Not only did he buy the part, but he also paid the mechanic to have it done the week that he was here before the graduation. Dan took care of the cost for all the food and drinks for the small celebration we had at my home before leaving for the cruise.

It was a three-day cruise out of Miami. We returned to Miami on Christmas Eve. My children, grandchildren, son-in-law, and I had a wonderful three days, and then spent another week in Miami, where we usually spent Christmas. I thought once again that everything was fine and we would have complete harmony with Dan and the children's relationships due to all the effort Dan made to only focus on his children. He left them with a feeling that they were the priority in his life once more.

My daughter made a comment one week later when Dan returned to Maryland. She made an observation and articulated it by saying, "When Dad was here for the graduation it felt like we had our old dad back, but as soon as he got back to Maryland he became the new dad."

That statement spoke volumes.

Two Steps Back

Dear Mistress Ali,

We began a new year, January 2013, my last semester before I graduated. My friend who lives in Rome with ovarian cancer was back out to work. It appeared that the chemotherapy and surgery might have worked. We were hopeful; there was no need for me to go to Rome quite as often. My children seemed to be in a better place since Dan was now in weekly communication with them. I felt, for the first time since the drama started, that my children were at peace and were open to continuing the relationship with their dad.

Everyone seemed okay until one day in early January when one of my son's friends stopped by. Apparently this friend worked at clubs in Atlanta where he did security

201

and had encountered your daughter enough times to establish a relationship with her. This young man had just come from Maryland and he attended the memorial service for your daughter. Because I have four children with one or two unusual, yet recognizable, names, this young man immediately realized that the paragraph in the program that stated the list of people left to "cherish her memory" were the names of my four children. He wanted to know why my son was not at the memorial for his stepsister. My son's jaw dropped in complete and utter dismay and bewilderment when he saw the program from the memorial service. This began a whole new rage for Kyle and Nick when they were told about the program. I was there to deal with all the anger and rage that the children felt yet again.

My kids were extremely upset since they did not know you, your children, your father, your sister, or anyone remotely connected with you. Why would you involve my children in your daughter's program, especially when you tried to suggest in your prior e-mail that my children cursed and threatened you? (Which never happened.) I do not get it. My eldest son actually wanted to call you that day and curse you out, but I stopped him. The papers and news stated that she was killed in a gang-related shooting; my children know nothing about gangs. My son did not want to be associated with her in any way, especially since he genuinely had no affiliation with her.

My four children were upset once more, because they could not understand how their dad could allow you to use their names, and for what reason? They blamed him because even though your daughter was well loved by her friends and family and had a brother and a grandfather who cherished her, why did you have to involve my children? I think you are mentally ill. I tried to tell the kids that maybe their dad had nothing to do with this, but on the program Dan was the one doing the welcoming and closing remarks. You had so much family that could have done it considering your daughter was twenty-one and Dan neither knew nor liked her. He has never said one positive thing about the child. I had such a hard time controlling the angry boys from calling you. I told them that I would handle it if they promised not to call you. They agreed.

I called Dan and asked him why he allowed you to use the children's name in your daughter's program. To my surprise, Dan had no clue what I was talking about. I proceeded to tell him what the children were upset about as one parent to another. He made it clear he knew nothing about that. I told him about the outrage that the boys felt, and he said he understood and that he would call me back. The kids did not believe his claim that he did not know, especially since he had such a starring role at the memorial service. So thanks to you the few forward steps that were made between Dan and the kids were now steps moving backward. I tried my best to plead Dan's case. I believed him due to my previous experience with how you operate. Dan called the kids and attempted to explain things to them. It did nothing to change their feelings.

In May 2013, despite the years of drama, illness, and pain, I laughed publicly yet cried privately. I experienced great sadness and loss at the passing of my brother-in-law in 2011, my dear friend's husband in 2012, and my friend with brain cancer in

February 2013, all while I was attending school. I managed to still emerge victorious. I was inducted as a member into the Phi Alpha International Honor Society in 2011. Omicron Gamma Phi Alpha Honor Society in 2012, and received my diploma in May 2013, graduating *magna cum laude*. My children, grandchildren, son-in-law, brothers, sisters, in-laws, and cousins from Canada were all present at the graduation, which was followed by a party organized by my children. My friends and family celebrated with me. Mistress Ali, you may have gotten my husband amidst mine and my kids' pain, but we are all still standing, happy, and loved. There is life after a divorce. I was employed less than one month after graduating. I took a break and started one month after accepting the position.

The New Dan

Dear Mistress Ali,

Sadly, "new Dan" is how my friends and family refer to Dan, and the children refer to him as the "new dad." You, Mistress Ali, would never understand why. The person that you describe as a "wonderful man" has been just that to anyone who knew him before you came into his life. You know nothing about the old Dan. Your idea of a wonderful man is distorted.

You think that a man married for over thirty years to his wife and had had four children with her and still proceeded to begin an affair with you anyway is a *wonderful man.*

This wonderful man came into your life; however, according to your sister, he told you "several scenarios" about his marital status when you met. He continuously gave different reasons to excuse his wife and four children at home. This *wonderful man,* in spite of having been a dad of four great kids, does not have any real relationship with any of his now adult children. This *wonderful man* not only cheated on his wife of over thirty years, but also treated her so badly in the end. Everyone looking on, not knowing the story, would be confused about who the unfaithful spouse was. This statement was even made by several of his former friends.

This *wonderful man* had a faithful wife who was good to him. She stuck with him through the good and bad times, through sickness and health. Yet still he abandoned her without a job, without a dime, and without caring what happened to her in the present or future.

This *wonderful man* had a life insurance policy that he pur-chased in 1989 for the purpose of taking care of his wife and children in the event of his death. The policy had a premium payment of only $75 per month. Approximately two months after moving to Maryland with you, without any discussion with his wife or consideration for his wife and children, this *wonderful man* cancelled the policy. Even though he left his wife without any form of income, he made sure that even if he were to have an untimely death his two children, still living at home, would not be financially okay.

This *wonderful man* lived with a wife who had a job with an airline. Despite this, he claimed to be deathly afraid of flying and deprived his tolerant wife and children of spending time with him when travelling around the world. Somehow he got over his fear when you helped him get the job he now has. This is a job that requires so much traveling that he gained thousands of frequent flyer miles within a short amount of time. I wonder if this *wonderful man* even stops to think how that makes his children feel.

This *wonderful man* despised your young daughter. Admittedly she may have been a challenge, but she was merely a kid who just needed love and attention. Although he married her mother, he made no real attempt to have any relationship with the child.

This *wonderful man* is such a liar to you that throughout your relationship with him he chose to ignore his children's pain regardless of how many times he was asked to try and heal his children. Yet you clearly were under the impression that "the children" were the ones responsible for healing the pain he allegedly felt.

This *wonderful man* loathed your own sister and described her as "bipolar drunk" each and every time he made a reference to her. This was whether he was speaking to me or anyone else about her.

This *wonderful man* made many efforts to appear as a great and wonderful dad. Four months before going to court for his divorce proceedings, for no apparent reason, he traded in our daughter's car. That car would have been paid off the following year, the same time she graduated from college. This man concocted a scheme to trade it in, although it was fine and only needed maintenance checkups, so that he could go before the judge and lie that her car was giving trouble and he had to buy her a new one. Therefore, according to him, he was unable to help me financially in any way as he now has the new car payment.

Fortunately my attorney spoke to Mia before court and discovered that her five-year-old Toyota Corolla, with 60,000 miles, worked fine. The court was not the least bit impressed with the "great daddy act" and ordered him to pay my mortgage until 2018. By which time he would be eligible to receive his Social Security benefits, making me eligible to receive one-half of his benefits. This is because I was his wife for over ten years. Since the divorce, as soon as our daughter graduated, this *wonderful man* began harassing his young daughter to take over the car payment.

This *wonderful man* came to Georgia to visit one year when Nick asked him to, as it was Father's Day weekend. The kids assumed that since you had your own father to stay and celebrate with he would be coming alone. They were wrong. This *wonderful man* spent the time talking to my son's new girlfriend about the rift between you and your own dad. That was supposedly why on Father's Day you were in a hotel room in Georgia by yourself while he was with his children for the first time in six years.

Since the year 2008, this *wonderful man* has not spent one Christmas, New Year's Day, Thanksgiving, or Easter with his children, nor they with him. This is because he has chosen you, his mistress, over his children and grandchildren. No one foresees any change in the future. How unfortunate for my family. This is all because you apparently do not trust him to be out of your sight and you are never welcomed around his kids or grandchildren.

This *wonderful man* is living a lie. The following are a few pieces of correspondence between Dan and me, Simone and her dad, and Dan and his friend. Please observe the dates, ranging from 2009 to 2012, where pleas were being made to Dan to love and communicate with his children. Some were from me, others are from friends and family. There are lots more like this, but printing all of them is not necessary. I think you'll get the point. So when you are pleading with my daughter to fix her dad, you are really confused.

Reply | Reply All | Forward | X Delete | Put in Folder ▼ | Print View | Save Address

From:
To:
Sent: Monday, January 10, 2011 3:54:43 PM
Subject: Indecent Exposure

HI Dan
It pains me that your family and former friends are faced with this reality. I have attached a picture of your beautiful children and grandchildren, all properly clad ladies and gentlemen, no indecent exposure, no body parts hanging out.
What a great group of kids, caring, loving and decent. Such a stark contrast to your newly found –step daughter-picture attached-proud of her academic under-achievement and her status of single motherhood at her tender age.
I can't imagine the Dan that I knew to be proud of that accomplishment. I sincerely hope that you realize what great kids you have and that you and their mother must have done something right and I hope that you attempt to honor that despite
your status with their mother. I really struggle with this whole thing-this place you have found yourself-is so foreign. I guess you must have found the kind of love that rocks your world entirely out of orbit-you must have fallen on your head.

From:
To:
Subject: FW: Follow Up
Date: Tues, 10 Feb 2009 14:44:11 +0000

Mom,
    I know you will be angry when you see what I did but I had to because I am just so fed up with Daddy.

Subject: Re: Follow Up
To:
From:
Date: Tue, 10 Feb 2009 13:40:28 +0000

Hi I don't know if you meant to send this to me but your dad's email is
_____. I did forward this to him. Sent via BlackBerry by AT&T

From:
Date: Tue, 10 Feb 2009 13:35:23 +0000
To:
Subject: Follow Up

Dad,
This is a follow up to the conversation we just had because I want to think that my father is a better man than he is but everytime you prove me wrong. Each time I call thinking maybe he will understand where I am coming from, what I am saying. Maybe if I remain calm you will see that things are really bad and take the blinders off. Everytime you prove me wrong.

Money, this is the number one killer of any relationship, and sadly it will be the undoing of ours. I want to save money to help support my new family yet but feel obligated to pick up the slack that you won't, and you don't care that's the part that hurts, and you have it, you can afford it more than I can..

You said you didn't disconnect from your family but you did. Tom went through a divorce too and yet he is still active in his children's life, he still supports them financially (even Andy who is the same age as Mia. He calls them, he thinks of things to do with them, you would rather retire your position as a parent.

210

You don't bother to help or do anything to extend support to your family, you don't even act like you like your children, your boys especially. Everyone rallies together for family except you. You would rather I take my last bit of savings, to help Kyle as a matter of fact, you would rather I go broke trying to support mom, someone who has supported you, just because you aren't in love anymore. You are not the first or last person to get a divorce and this could be more amicable if you extend yourself a little more. Tom has gone above and beyond for Kim (wife of 1 year) and kids, especially financially but now she is back on her feet and doesn't need him for anything. That's how divorce should work, not your callus example. I wouldn't treat my worse enemy the way you did my mother. Keep telling yourself that you are doing everything and that you have done more than enough. I am a fair person and I am telling you, you haven't, not even close.

I find it hard to believe that you don't have $300 in your account to aid your child. That you are more strapped for cash than me who just had a child, starting a career and paying off medical expenses. You know that when you die you can't take your money with you right.

But you are right like you said it is my choice to help them because I don't have to, but I will because mommy is all I have, my family is all I have. This stress is killing mom and I want to do everything to prevent that. My friend's mom just died at age 55 and that's who helped raise her child. I do not want that to be my reality. I know this is falling on deaf ears because at no point will you ever say maybe just maybe I need to step in. Maybe I can offer a little. The less you have to do the happier you are. I wish I could have that peace of mind.

📤 | 📥 | ↪   ⬆ | ⬇ | ✕ | 📋 Inbox

📤 Reply | 📤 Reply All | ↪ Forward | ✕ Delete | 📁 Put in Folder ▾ | 🖨 Print View | 💾 Save Address

From:
To:
Subject:
Date: Thu, 27 May 2010 08:11:35 -0400

Hi Dan

It is so weird that after 38 years of knowing you and four children together I can only communicate with you in writing, that is okay though. I also do not know if you would care but I just thought I would let you know that Yvonne_____ passed away.

Eva-Marie

Dan, since I have no axe to grind at this point and I am still concerned about the well being of our children, I am BEGGING you to please do not say anything about me to the children, it does not help YOU in any way. It does not affect ME AT ALL but it sure is working AGAINST you, your children grew to adulthood in this home with their two parents, they saw and knew the life we had with them, stop trying to convince them of anything different. You may not believe this, but there is nothing left for you to do to me, I have accepted what you have done and I wish you and Ali _____ a happy life together, I hope you can find peace and happiness in your new life and your new surroundings with your new family.I pray for that for you everyday.

I truly have no animosity towards you and Ali anymore, god and my therapist has taken care of me in everyway that matters. My children are a different matter, it almost would have been easier for them if we had a bad marriage and you were a dead beat father their whole life, but as you and I both know that was never the case. I pray everyday that you can open your heart to find a way to get some help or advice on how to fix you kids, they are all full of ANGER and HATE and I am forced to deal with this by myself even though I am not the person they have issues with. Trying to call or calling them on the phone and acting as if the past four years did not happen is not helping. This is just my humble advice in an effort to mend the relationship between you and your children (as that is the only thing I want in life right now). Making every effort to communicate with them…acknowledge what you have done to their family and to them…APOLOGIZE TO THEM…and ACCEPTING whatever rage, hate or anger that they may exhibit is a start.

If you care you can take my advice…if you don't, it is okay, it is not about ME. I LOVE my kids and want to help them be whole again and get rid of all that anger and I think you should care too. If you are not ready to do this, so be it…I will continue to pray that one day you will. Be safe and have a good day.

Love

🡄 | 🡇 | ✕ | 📇 Inbox

Reply | Reply All | Forward | ✕ Delete | Put in Folder ▾ | Print View | Save Address

From:
To:
Subject:
Date: Tue, 26 Oct 2010 08:15:32 -0400

Hi Dan

I received this thing you sent me in the mail, I guess I should thank you,
what a pity that Simone was at the house when
I received it. Dan as I told you before, if you do not fix your children, you
will be alone in this world and I think you deserve
more than that for yourself. Just to let you know, Simone has had a notion
in her head for over a year now, that if I spoke
to you in a "particular way" that you will be different with me. As a result
the last three times I have spoken to you it has
been in Simon's presence so when you continue to tell her that I am
always cussing and carrying on when I speak to you
guess what you look like to Simone? You are not doing anything to me but
you are hurting yourself and your children. I am so over
you and the life you have chosen for yourself, what reason could I possibly
have to curse or carry on with you? I am not even angry with you anymore,
the only thing I feel for you is great sadness. Everytime I look at our two
BEAUTFIL PRECIOUS grandchildren
I feel sad for you. Everytime I am in Florida and people who loved you
soooo much are still hurting at your abandonment of them, I feel
sad for you. Everytime our children and grandchildren are at the house or
in Florida with me, I feel sad for you. When I attended your
niece's wedding and saw the love given to Ken at his daughter's wedding
and the care given to him because he is in a wheelchair,
I felt sad for you. So please tell me why will I be cussing or yelling at you?
You don't have your grandchildren, your friends, your culture
your children, even your own family, so again I ask, why will I be cussing
you? I pray for you everyday that your children will find it in their
heart to forgive you if you ever need them. Forget what you did to me, you
chose Ali's family over YOUR OWN CHILDREN and GRANDCHILDREN,
you chose her parents, her children, her GRANDCHILD, her sister, her
friends over YOUR OWN, which causes such pain to your children, you
made that choice, not me, the problems created in Simon's relationship
with T (which she will NEVER tell you) were created by YOU, not ME. I no
longer have any reason to be cussing you, those days are over. I know
you will consider yourself to be
happy, but trust me when I tell you, until you hear the sweet voice of your
grandchild say "I love you Mimi" while her little arm is around
your neck in the bed, you don't know happiness. Ask your girlfriend, she'll
tell you what it feels like!!!!! I hope this puts an end to you

repeating the nonsense. One more thing Dan, please stop denying the fact that it is your extra-martial affair that destroyed your marriage. If it was not that, please let me know what it was, I think anyone who has ever know us will also like to know what other
reason there was, I am certainly in the dark as to what else it could have been, please shed some light on the reason for me please.

Dan I have a test today, So i cannot waste anymore time writing you, especially when I suspect that all of this is going in one eye and out the next. If only you will let me help you fix your children before you need them. Trust me, YOU WILL one day and that girlfriend of yours
could not care less about your relationship with your kids and grandkids, she sure cares about hers, take a page out of her book. LOVE YOUR KIDS AND GRANDKIDS while you can and SHOW IT not just SAY IT. Action speaks louder than words.

One more thing, apparently Simone will do anything to make you speak to me,(I just found that out) let me help you with that. Don't
Bother. I really do not see the point anymore of speaking to you NOW or AFTER we are divorced. If you did not see the necessity of speaking to me all this time, do not make anymore make you do something you do not want to do. I have spoken to Simone she will be okay. It is sad that after 35 years of a marriage we are reduced to e-mails, YOUR choice.If I absolutely must tell you something I will do just what I am doing now send, you and e-mail. So Dan take care of yourself,try to be happy, and remember you have a beautiful family here in Georgia who have done you nothing. Be Blessed.
Love

_____

Reply | Reply All | Forward | X Delete | Put in Folder ▼ | Print View | Save Address

From:
To:
Subject: FW: indecent exposure
Date: Tue, 18 Jan 2011 23:08:54 -0500

Dan

In case you would like me to send this to your mistress, go ahead and hang up the phone on me again. I am entitled to be frustrated dealing with all the issues that the children are having, while you pretend they do not exist. I AM FRUSTRATED with the life you have forced me to have because you chose to move on to OTHER PASTURES because I can assure you they are not GREENER. You broke up your marriage because you had an affair. What part of that is not true? Continue to deny it and we will hear what your mistress's opinion is after I send her some cards you sent me in 2006. Or can I send her the video with your speech about your wonderful family. For Christ sake ADMIT what you have done and move on. Start the healing process with your children. Let me know when Kyle can move to DC with you, I hope soon, it may be before you think you are ready. I am sure that I have had ENOUGH. A plane ticket is all he needs, what will you do when he arrives? throw him out? What a great father you will be.

🖎 | 🖎 | 🖎   ⬀ | ⬦ | ✕ | 🖾 Inbox

🖎 Reply | 🖎 Reply All | 🖎 Forward | ✕ Delete | 🖎 Put in Folder ▾ | 🖎 Print View | 🖎 Save Address

From:
Date: September 11, 2012 at 11:10:39 AM PDT
To:

Dan

You know I made a vow to myself since my life is so happy, to not inject negative stuff into it, however, it is just truly amazing to me that day after day you can live without your two most precious grandchildren. Today was grandparent's day in Olivia's school for the second year in a row, the only difference is, this time she asked if grandpa was coming. My heart breaks for her and Chris, you would have soooo enjoyed YOUR grandchildren, instead you are busy playing house with someone elses grandchildren.Soooooooo Sad. I feel so sad for Simone especially since she loved you sooooo very much and feels that you would have been the best grandfather of all, however she deals with it by telling herself, "you chose what was most important to you and it was not your children or grandchildren it was your mistress/wife and her family" don't waste your time trying to convince them differently. I have tried, but your kids are grown, smart, mature and understand that there is no defense for your behavior and the funny thing is, it has nothing to do with me and what you did to me, it is about what you did to them. Everyday is a struggle for me to try and help my children to cope with being abandoned by their father, you would think that after all this time that they would be better but quite frankly I think as time goes and occasions arise like (lunch with grandparents) they only feel worst. I pray that each and every one of them can get the necessary help to clear their hearts of the pain they feel. I pray that god can help your children to forgive you so they can all free themselves of their different emotions of hate, anger, rage and pain that they continue to harbor in their soul, I pray for them everyday and ask god to give me the health, strength and patience to continue to be a loving and patient mother and to be there for them as long as possible since I am the only parent they have. I will ask you once again, get some professional help, tell the truth about what you did and try and fix your children before it is too late. I hope you get this e-mail, I was told you have a new e-mail address, Aliguy@aol.com I will not be using that one, sorry!!!

Having stated all of the above, my standards of a *wonderful man* are much, much higher than yours, obviously. The old Dan was a *wonderful man* but "the new Dan," based on your standards, is considered a prize. For those of us who have known him all his adult life thus far, we cheer you on as you walk away with your "booby prize."

Part II

Letters to the Husband

To My Cheating Husband,

I saw you as my hero.
I saw you as part of my heart.
Never thought this love would end
Until death do us part.

Thirty-six years of marriage
I gave you all I had.
Thirty-six years of love and support
Through the good and the bad.

We raised four wonderful children
An accomplishment we shared.
Amidst strict discipline and tough rules
Our love for them went unimpaired

You were not the perfect husband
You were not the perfect dad
You did the best with what you knew
Since that was all you had.

For everyone in your inner circle, family and friends,
The hole you left within their hearts
Seems impossible to mend.

The pain you caused your loved ones
Seemed to be completely over your head.
You have no knowledge, you have no clue
Seems that the guy we once knew is dead.

You show no remorse for your actions
You do not seem to care.
I promise you the day will come
When you will be crippled by the burden you have to bear.

So now I begin a new chapter in my life
And you are no longer in it.
The heartache has gone, the joy has returned
And I do not miss you one bit.

You married your mistress and hoped for marital bliss.
It is hard for me to comprehend
That you both can expect this.
Marital woes seem to be a more realistic expectation
Since the foundation of your relationship was built
While creating devastation.

For now I say I wish you well
because in your future or your afterlife
You will experience hell

Dear Father,

Where do I begin? There are so many things I would like to say but I am instructed to keep it short. I will start by saying that I cannot believe that the person we relied on to be leader of our family is the person responsible for destroying it. It was bad enough that you had an affair but the way you handled the whole situation was reprehensible. You first started by making my little sister out to be a liar by denying that she heard you on the phone talking to your mistress, when in fact you were the one lying the entire time, and I do mean the entire time. What kind of father does that to their young daughter? A coward, that's who.

Cheating is never a good thing, but I think you and Mom may have been able to work things out had you taken responsibility for your actions and got some help to work through the situation. Worst-case scenario, if it could not have been worked out at least you and Mom could have remained cordial with each other. Instead you abandoned not just Mom, but also your four children, two grandchildren, and all your friends and family. Regardless of my feelings toward you, Mom always tried to convince me to treat you with respect as my dad. How could I respect a dad who had an affair and exposed his fifteen-year-old daughter to it, lied on his own daughter, slapped his young daughter in her face, and took a gun out on his two sons who attempted to come to her defense?

Prior to this affair and the destruction of our family, I did respect you as a father and a husband and a man who provided for his family. You have now lost all the respect I had for you over the years because in the end you showed no regard for your family in anyway, financially or otherwise. You allowed your mistress and her family to disrespect your wife and your children and you did nothing. That was when it became clear to me that you were a coward, and that you didn't give a damn about your family. I could never respect someone like that. I thank God every day for my uncle Allan, who has always been there for me, before during and after the drama that you created.

I am somewhat thankful for you though. You did show me every way a man should not treat his kids, his family, and the people he claims he cares about. I can honestly go on and on with this letter, but what is the point? If after all this time you haven't and don't get it, I don't think you ever will. I will say this though, the day you become a real man, grow a pair, and you want to have a real honest conversation, let me know.

The man you're not,

Your son

To my dad,

For most of my life we have been close. Everyone who knows me knows I was proud to be born a day after your birthday and call myself your daughter. I always believed that we shared similar traits of loyalty, confidence, helpfulness, determination, and a caring heart. As my father, I could depend on you if I needed anything, no matter how small or how large the request.

I remember a time when I got stranded on the road because of car trouble. You left your job, which was in the opposite direction from where I was, fought rush-hour traffic, to come and assist me, all while keeping me calm. The next day I told that story to a friend, beaming about how blessed I was to have such a great dad come rescue me, and she remarked, "Why don't you just get AAA?" I remember telling her that funnily enough the thought never crossed my mind, because you were my AAA. Why would I pay some random service when I had a dad willing and able to help me with whatever I needed?

You were the parent I felt most comfortable calling on if I needed help with my car or had heavy lifting to do, needed repairs, financial advice, or just to vent about a situation Mom couldn't help me with. Because you were so constant in my life, I never grew up with daddy issues or feeling like I needed someone else to take care of me. You were a great role model for me and a man I would measure all my boyfriends and eventually my husband up against.

When I got married, I thought I had the recipe for a great marriage because I had seen it modeled by you and Mom for so many years. So imagine my horror when all my beliefs came crashing down in 2006, a year into my marriage, due to your infidelity. Not only did you cheat but you also showed a general lack of concern for everyone involved except yourself and your mistress. The great husband and father I once knew was now a selfish and hurtful individual with his own agenda, in complete juxtaposition to your former self.

Your affair left me broken. I was confused by your actions and blatant disregard for your kids, my kids, and your estranged wife. As a wife myself, I took so many things you did prior to and after the divorce personally. Both you and Mom raised me to be a strong individual and to stand up for myself, yet you tried to weaken my mother with your hatefulness. It didn't make any sense to me. This was not the guy I knew. The father I knew showed me how a man was supposed to treat me.

I remember past Christmases and birthdays where you would take both Mia and me on the hunt for the perfect gift for Mom because you felt she deserved the best. And now, because of your lustful pre-occupation with someone else, Mom didn't even deserve so much as a Mother's Day phone call.

As your child I was angry too. I was angry that my husband never really got to see the kind of loving and devoted husband you were years prior. He never got to see our family complete and whole and loving. Instead all you showed him was how to cheat on your wife and get away with it by any means necessary.

Did you think that your actions were appropriate to impart on your newly wedded daughter and son-in-law? My husband had very few older men in his life to model how to be a husband on. His dad died before he could show him, so I counted on you to lead the way and you failed me. You never even gave me a thought or considered how your actions would impact my life, my marriage, during this whole ordeal. That speech you gave to my husband before we got married about treating me right and honoring me is so comical now in light of your own transgressions.

Thanks to your affair, I question everything—my husband, the longevity of my marriage, the age-old adage about a happy ever after. Mom has tried several times to remind me that every marriage is different and her fate will not be mine. But while I pray it won't happen, I am not sure if I truly believe her yet. I am still dealing with the aftermath of your divorce. The simple truth that there is no Mom and Dad cooking in the kitchen for Thanksgiving, no Mom and Dad to watch my kids for a weekend, no trips to Florida as a complete family—hell, I am still dealing with the fact that we aren't a complete family—means we are forever displaced.

In recent years, we have been working toward a better relationship, a relationship I resisted at first but can now appreciate, partly because I get to see glimpses of the dad I used to know, the dad that was devoted to his kids and concerned about their wellbeing. I also see flashes of the grandfather I always dreamed you would be to my children. Of course there are other fractions of you that still remind me what you are capable of, stubborn and cold, especially as it relates to other family members. But I keep praying for you, hoping the good in you will prevail before it's too late. So that's where I am now, hoping and praying . . . and surviving.

Dan,

I call you Dan because I no longer view the person that you have become as any kind of father. To begin with, the "father" that you used to be was not all that great in itself. However, I knew no better, so I don't hold it against you as much as your most recent disgusting behavior. With that being said, you should still be made aware of it.

Growing up, the time before I hit my teenage years was okay, I must say. You were a big jungle gym for my friends and me, and everything you did was cool. You came to a few basketball games. From your height and strength to your pocket knife to your handyman skills, I wanted to be like that guy when I grew up. And some of those traits have stuck with me to this day, so I give you credit for that.

Back then, in my eyes you and Mom were the perfect, old-fashioned but balanced couple. Dad did man things; Mom did woman things, with the occasional compromise. Dad worked, Mom was the homemaker. Dad cut the grass and fixed the car; Mom washed the clothes and cooked the food. I still believe in that today, and as a result I treat women well and have sought after values. Again, I give you credit for that.

Once I moved on from that phase of my life where you were somewhat idolized, I came into my teenage years. I started forming my own opinions on life and choices that I would make. This is the point where our relationship started to change. It seemed to me that you didn't like the fact that I no longer hung onto your every word, and because of this you started to treat me differently. The fun side was fading, and what was left was an overly stern father who barely knew how to crack a smile.

I had friends my age and their fathers just seemed to embrace them getting older and they got along well still. What made things worse is that when my friends were around you got along with them so well also.

For this reason it was hard to tell if it was me that was the issue, so I struggled back and forth with that thought.

When I complained to my mother about things, she would say that that's exactly how her father had been and that's just the way it was. She would tell me that parents aren't supposed to be your friends. I understood that, but still I felt like it didn't have to be so cut and dry. However, I knew no better and I trusted my mother.

So life continued in that manner, you silent and stern except when people other than family were around. Holiday time when family visited was awesome. You made jokes, you laughed, you would ruffle up my hair and ask, "You all right, boy?" when I walked by, just like my friends' dads.

To jump ahead, fresh in my twenties is when you apparently started cheating on Mom and things took a turn for the worst. You weren't even just sour anymore, you were vindictive and did things intentionally to hurt. You purposely picked fights with me and always threatened to physically injure me. There was even a time you asked me on Friday night to cut the grass at some point Saturday. However, when I woke up at 10:00 a.m. you had already done it. Then to add insult to injury you came and screamed at me for not having it done!

You were just an unhappy person until Mom would go out of town. You would disappear for lengthy periods of time. I don't know if it was that you thought we were telling her something, considering we knew nothing at that time, but like clockwork, a few days after her return it was attitude from you for days. This is when I formed my own opinion of what you were doing. I was not a child, and I could see with my own eyes what was going on. I knew something was up but I had no proof, so I kept it to myself.

My little sister and I always thought a lot alike. One day we were talking and she had a very confused look on her face. She appeared to be struggling with something. Finally I got her to say a little bit of what she was thinking. She said, "I kinda think Dad might . . ." I finished the sentence for her. I knew she was trying to suggest you were having an affair, because it was what I already believed anyway. Once that came out and you and Mom were going through whatever, you treated me worse than you did ever before. You didn't speak, you lived in a separate room, and there was a permanent frown on your face.

Despite all of this and what was occurring with my mother, I still appeased you when you decided to have a good day. I even used to cut your hair when you asked, but when my clippers broke while cutting my friend's hair, you wouldn't let me use yours in order to finish the cut so I wasn't late for work. You told me to fix them. You were just plain mean. When my mother sided with me on that argument and was upset with you for not letting me use them, you cursed me, tried to fight me and choke me, but luckily I was not small and it was not an easy thing for you to do though I never actually fought back. I simply defended myself and pushed you away from me. You didn't speak to me for months. You walked up and down in the same house with me, and when my birthday came you wouldn't even speak to me to say happy birthday (one of the few things you did as a father should).

At this point you are the person still cheating on my mother but you're behaving as if we did something to you. You slapped my little sister, and when my brother and I came to see what was going on and asked you not to hit her again, you pulled a gun on us.

When you finally separated from my mother, nothing changed. Despite the fact that you had the woman and life you obviously wanted, you continued to do malicious things to us. I already withdrew from college, where I was a walk on-to the football team at Valley State, so I could come home and help Mom. I needed to do so because you stopped paying the bills without warning. Every month was something else: lights cut, the water, then cable. There were times we had to shower using a bucket of hot water from the stove. Who does things like that to their family all for another woman?

In no way, shape, or form do I agree with what you have done. It's disgusting to begin with; however, as my mother even said, she could get over the actual cheating and she was the one you wronged. At that point my brother and I tried to come to you from a man's point of view and asked you to just tell the truth and be nice to Mom. We both had seen other men, some very close to us, make the same mistake and step outside their marriage, but their family always came first no matter what. You were still denying any wrongdoing. To this day you have never admitted to actually cheating or the other wrong things you did.

That is why I do not respect you. That is why now you are not even a man to me. You are absolutely nothing to me. I feel nothing for you. I wish no harm on anybody, but I can assure you if something unfortunate were to befall you I would be the last place you need to look to for help. With that being said, I think it is pretty clear where you stand with me. You are just some worthless man named Dan I used to kind of know. The person I called Dad at one point started fading when I was a teen and completely disappeared once this thing you now call your wife came into the picture. So you two will continue on.

I do not wish you happiness as I couldn't care less what happens to either of you. As you can see, whether you want to admit it or not, karma has already started coming for your behinds in the form of drama, family resentment, and even death. I know you know what I mean, and I know that crazy, manipulative, ghetto, gutter slut you call wife knows it too.

You losers deserve any and everything coming to you. Enjoy hell, you bastard. My conscience is clear. Good riddance.

Your son

Dad,

Sometimes when my life gets hard I remember I have a father. This is someone who is partially responsible for my wellbeing. If the situation is dire enough, maybe I'll get some semblance of compassion and kind words. If you happen to be in a good mood, it is possible that you will help enough to make a difference in my already downtrodden circumstances. Yet, still, I've never seen your paternal instincts fully kick in. I've never seen the storybook father come in to "save the day." At least, not without potentially creating a bigger issue first.

When things are going really well in my life, I don't think to call you and share. I've never truly gotten the feeling that my being well or not matters to you. On your list of priorities, if something is not threatening to my existence or somewhat beneficial to you, it is low, if even on the list. This is how I expect most things in my life relative to yours. I feel neglected and taken for granted.

Logically some things are not worth sharing with you. If I am sick, you'll remind me to drink plenty of fluids. I don't know if you care that sometimes I cannot even afford said fluids. If something is wrong with the car you love to hold over my head, you're not around to see to it that mechanics don't take advantage of me. But then, with property in your name you demonstrate a tad more interest in its maintenance.

I do appreciate your investment(s) in my education. You helped with the cosigning of my loans so that I could earn my degree at a very prestigious university. But even then, to be completely honest, I wonder if it is just so that you can finally let go of the remaining obligations I have burdened you with. I have large goals and dreams for my career, not because of you, but in spite of you.

As I grow older I realize that I will never have the "daddy" my sister had. You taught her how to drive a manual car; you taught me how to notice red flags in my relationships. You moved her into college; I learned how to pack and move efficiently to alleviate the stress from my mother when moving five times in my four-and-a-half collegiate years. You walked my sister down the aisle; I don't even know if I want your immoral presence in the sacred church that will bless my union. Her children know and love you; I can only hope that my future husband will have a father so my future children can be guaranteed at least one grandfather.

I still remember watching To Sir, with Love with you and Mom in your bed as a child. I must've been no older than nine or ten. Since then I always knew our daddy/daughter dance would be to that song. I would want to dedicate it to the man who took me from "crayons to perfume." What I didn't know then was that you would not be a large enough presence to have a positive impact on my rearing. Now the song that reminds me of you is "Love the Way You Lie" by Eminem. The song starts,

> *Just gonna stand there and watch me burn*
>
> *That's all right because I like the way it hurts*
>
> *Just gonna stand there and hear my cry*
>
> *That's all right because I love the way you lie,*
>
> *Love the way you lie.*

Hi Dan,

It is not with warm feelings that I eventually got the strength to put pen to paper to address your behavior, which I am still convinced that you were not capable of exhibiting. I truly believe that something or somebody interfered with your mind to bring about such drastic changes.

Dan, I met you more than forty years ago and we immediately became good friends then best of friends, which I believe happened because you and I were both highly regarded by our good friend Ernest and we therefore trusted and respected each other from day one, no screening was necessary.

Throughout the many years of friendship, I, like Ernest, thought you were one hell of a friend, husband, father, son-in-law, brother-in-law, uncle, uncle-in-law, and in general, like everyone who knew you thought you were a decent human being and cherished their association with you.

It has crossed my mind as to whether the Dan we all knew and loved for forty-plus years was a fake and what we see now is the real Dan, but I don't think it is possible for someone to pretend for that length of time, so again I am convinced that something or somebody evil happened to you. And I am not an awfully superstitious person, but I strongly believe where there is good, there is bad/evil.

My friend Dan could never neglect his home, his wife, his children, his grandchildren, his brothers, his sisters, his many nieces and nephews, his friends, his country, his culture, his food, his music, his traditions, his hobbies, give up his job that he loved, move to a cold place, and all this for what? To be a fourth husband to someone clearly not of his social status? (There is no prize for fourth.) To live in her father's basement? To have a new job that he hates and which involves travelling by plane, of which he is deathly afraid? To be an in-law to people who do not like him and view

234

him as an island man who cannot speak English? To be a step grandfather to a baby whose mother was shot due to her reckless, irresponsible, destructive lifestyle? Who is this creature and where is my friend?

Dan, let me remind you just in case that part of your memory is also shot. I have gone through a separation, divorce, and a new marriage just like you and many, many others, some of whom we know personally. But believe me when I say I have never, never heard of anyone doing what you have done. And I know people who have done a lot of destruction in and out of their marriage but I have never ever heard of a story that can be compared to yours.

You have created a lot of hurt and irreparable damage to both your immediate and extended family, but I am a Christian, so will not wish you any further harm, but I am not Christian enough to wish you well. You need to repent, ask the Lord's forgiveness and maybe one day we may be friends again in another life.

Your ex-friend and brother-in-law

To my ex-brother-in-law,

When asked if I wanted to write you a letter, I said yes at first. I thought I had so much to say to you about how many lives you altered by your immoral, cowardly, despicable behavior. How you sat back and allowed your mistress and her sister to disrespect, curse, threaten, and intimidate my sister, my nieces, and my nephews for no reason. How you abandoned your children and grandchildren by moving to another state, knowing that they could not visit you. They did not even know where you were living. How you moved into the home of your mistress's father and his wife and was so comfortable living in their basement. How you allowed my sister to be harassed by creditors looking for your newfound family members until I was forced to put a stop to it.

What man permits all this to be inflicted on his family because he decided to have a mistress? None that I know. You are not worth my time or my energy. You are the biggest loser that I know. I am sure you will have a miserable life.

Your ex-brother-in-law

Dear Dan,

I remember at your twenty-fifth wedding anniversary how I surprised everyone, including myself, when I stepped out of character to speak in public. I had shared a home with you all for many months and I wanted to tell family and friends what a wonderful example you two were as a couple. I had seen what a considerate and thoughtful husband you were and I knew you to be a very devoted father to some very happy children.

Your in-laws, of which I am one, have always considered you to be the best. You were reliable, dependable, and helpful in any situation. We relied not only on your physical strength, which was legendary, but also on the emotional strength that you exhibited.

Your family of origin also loved you greatly and you deserved their love. You were a hero to your nieces and nephews and a great support to your sisters. If those praises sound too much, they are not. To borrow a modern phrase, Dan, "You were all that."

When I first heard about your affair, all that said to me was that you are human and imperfect. I imagined that the marriage had slipped off the tracks as most marriages do over the course of time. Because of my experience of you and your marriage relationship, I fully expected that the internal issues would be resolved and that you would see your "mistake" and be reconciled with your wife. Sadly, I was wrong.

I did not lose faith in you even when you left your home and you abandoned your families. By that I mean not just your own wife and children but your sisters, your nieces and nephews, all of your in-laws, and some of your closest friends. Even when you abandoned your life, so to speak, I could not and would not abandon you. I was sure that there was a force directing you away from love and responsibility that you were unable to control. In the circumstances I did what I always do: I prayed. I dedicated a rosary for you every single day for a very long time. As you know, I also took the opportunity to contact you at least once a year on your birthday. I wanted you to know that I was one door that was still open if you needed to find you way back to us.

I know now that whatever took you away from us has changed you so much that you will never be able to think of coming back, and sadly, we don't want you back. We lost you, we grieved you, we have moved on without you. I don't wish you ill, but I know that because of the order in the universe that our Creator made, even if someday you too are able to move on (I know you haven't yet) I know that you will never be happy.

Best Regards

Your ex-sister-in-law

Dear Dan,

It's been awhile since last I saw you or even had a chance to speak with you over the past seven years. I have often times been given to occasional reflection on how this unfortunate sequence of estrangement came to pass, and always a feeling of sadness comes over me.

I think about the times we shared, the fun, the laughter, the cama- raderie, and the happy moments at holidays, special events, children's milestones, etc. You were a brother-in-law by common standards but in actual fact you were my brother. I loved and respected you in what you stood for, your honesty, your integrity, your decency, and your general affability. You were an excellent husband to my sister and a loving, faithful, and committed father. And now I muse to myself, "Whatever happened to my brother and my friend?"

In my entire life I have witnessed other breakups, but I have never seen anything that compares, even remotely, to the pestilence that was visited upon you. Yes, men have left their wives, but I know of no one who in parting separated themselves from and given up their wives, their children, grandchildren, their brothers, their sisters, their friends, their culture, and their way of life. There is no woman, past or present, who could have exacted such a high price from me to be with her, and quite candidly, I don't think that the woman you met, with the little I know of her, is worthy of the sacrifice you have made.

Dan, I am almost certain that the day will come when you will look around you and realize that you made a grave mistake and was robbed in the exchange.

I still see your family often enough, and every time I think, "How could Dan be at peace with himself missing all of this?" We still celebrate the triumphs and successes of your children. You have two absolutely adorable grandchildren and it hurts me to think that they are growing up without the benefit of truly knowing their grandfather.

When you and my sister celebrated your twenty-fifth wedding anniversary, no one could have envisaged that five years later you and your beloved wife would end this way. Pray, Dan, that the blinders would fall from your eyes and that one day soon you would be reconciled with all the people you have forsaken. In the meantime, I'll keep you in my prayers.

Your ex-brother-in-law

Dear Dan,

It is heart-wrenching any time a marriage ends, especially one like yours that had so many years invested in it. I often thought to myself that the closeness you all shared as a family was the epitome of everything beautiful; something I searched for, an example I wanted to follow.

You and Eva were great friends to my husband, and, Dan, you were our marriage counselor! I always remember calling you for advice in times of trouble and you never once hesitated to help. So my questions for you are: What happened? Where did this great guy go? Where did this devoted husband and father go? Why? Why? Why? We are left alone with only our unanswered questions to keep us company.

I am not here to judge you but to give you some advice that you would have given to me. You were wrong! What you did to your beautiful family is definitely not advice you would have given me, and if you did, I would not have taken it.

I grasp this opportunity to write to you since I tried you on a few occasions and you totally ignored me. I want you to know that I am not taking sides but I have heard Eva's side and I have personally experienced some of the harassment she received on the job. And so I ask you, what could possibly have happened? How could something that seemed so right go so wrong? Why couldn't this be worked out? Wasn't it worth it, especially for the beautiful and adorable kids that you have? I just can't understand why. One lesson I have learned about betrayal is that it never comes from your enemies!

Take care, Dan, and as we say back home, "Walk good!" God Bless!

Your ex-friend

Hi Dan

What's up? We have not connected for quite a while, so I thought I should write, as believe it or not this year 2014 is fifty years, yes, fifty years since we entered high school. This should be a significant celebration; however, we are scattered so far and wide it is proving difficult to organize any meaningful celebration. Many who reside in North America are still employed. We here in this twin-island named after God himself are blessed to have retired, and enjoying every moment of it, two years ago. We could still go down memory lane on those five years we spent in high school, and what a journey it was.

I cannot think of one person in the entire school who did not know that you were a gentleman, always well groomed, respectful, and intelligent. And these qualities were complemented by your stature. Yogi Carlton fell head over heels in love with these qualities and she had every right to. What a catch! We were blessed to be taught by teachers who loved and disciplined us as if we were their own. Others provided us with humor. Remember Mr. O'Lara's "take d fence" when you were put out of class for misbehaving. Oops, sorry, you never suffered that disgrace. You were always well behaved, a trait that many of us at that time would make fun of; however, we soon began to value someone as well rounded as you.

My last memory of you at school was at our school's graduation. Oh what a night. You stood at the podium and delivered the valedictorian speech with clarity, passion, and a bit of sadness. Do you have a copy of that speech? I would really like to hear it again. How proud your children must be. How many of us could testify that our father was the valedictorian? Sadly, not many.

Our paths met again in the Big Apple as you were dating my sister's in-law. I was pleased to have met up with a school friend, and did we have "good times." Remember the saying that we made famous? "If work interfering with your time, forget the work." The Labor Days on Western Crescent distributing roti to all and sundry. Going to the nation's capital in the Turkey and breaking down about five times before arriving at our destination. The rides on the Cyclone in Coney Island. These are memories that we could never forget.

Then came your big day. Yes, your marriage to the girl of your dreams, Eva. I felt honored to be part of the bridal party and it was truly a grand affair, although Eva's godfather promised that if you do not treat her well, "The vengeance of Moko would fall on you."

You and the family returned home and our friendship continued. Your role as husband and father was one to be truly admired. You provided for your family not only materially, but in every aspect of life. You braided your daughter's hair. Not many men would feel comfortable with that privilege, but you could not care what others thought. You did it out of "agape" love for your child. Remember those Saturday times at Tyrico? How could we forget those days, riding the waves. Carnival, yes, from Panorama (toting coolers after the incident) to carnival Tuesday night, we celebrated carnival to the fullest: tents, fetes, playing mats, we did it all and enjoyed every moment.

Well, Dan, I kept inquiring about you from your wife and the answers were always vague; e.g., "You know Dan, he's OK." Or, "He is not with us on this trip as he is afraid of airplanes." This totally shocked me, as when I saw your wife and children the group always looked so incomplete without you. What was happening? After some time passed, I was informed by your wife that things were not going well with you guys and she was thinking of filing for a divorce due to your infidelity. Oh no, this could not be true, not Dan, who had eyes for no one else but Eva. Eva — wife and mother par excellence, who kept the family together through the good and bad times, who forgave and when she remembered forgave again. This could not be happening. Sadly, it was. I know you must be saying that every story has two sides and I have not heard your side. Yes, that's true, but I quote Sparrow: "Sixteen million French men cannot be wrong."

Dan, are you the same person who came to school on Spanish Street in Woodstock fifty years ago? Or have you been "transformed" (for want of a better word) into someone who your family and friends can no longer identify? Is what Uncle Eric promised you at your wedding really happening? I await your response. I pray that you reflect on your life today and truthfully affirm if this is what you saw forty years ago. Jesus heals. Speak to him truthfully and he will minister to you in ways you cannot imagine. It's not too late.

Aunty

My friend,

We go way back as friends and buddies. The reason we shared such a bond was because we had so much in common. We had wives whom we loved, we had kids we would die for, we confided in each other, we kept secrets for each other, and overall we had morals, values, and great work ethic. We were providers for our families and we were heads of our households. Our wives loved us and so did our children. We were not perfect. We make stupid mistakes as most husbands do. We were often misunderstood. We had ups and downs in our marriages but we hung in there because the ups significantly outnumbered the downs. I respected you and your opinion because you were married longer than I was and you seemed to have a good grasp on what it took to keep you family together.

The words to express how I feel about what you have done are inadequate. I am incapable of expressing my feeling on the matter for several reasons.

1. As close as we had been, your mistress was a well-kept secret. That fact alone causes me to wonder. I defended you when I first heard of it because I was sure that it was just gossip, because I just knew you would have shared that with me. You know I would never have judged you. I have always had your back and you mine.

2. At no point in our friendship and as husbands did I ever hear you say anything about you wife that would have ever alerted me that there was a major or serious problem in your marriage. You guys were my example of a real marriage.

3. For you to discard our friendship without any warning or ex-planation makes me empathize with your wife and children. Only God knows how traumatizing this must be for them.

4. I have such diminished respect for you when I see what you have done to your family, and worst of all, you continue to try to encourage a relationship between us and your new wife. Sorry to say, anyone who knew you and your beautiful family would never disrespect your ex-wife by encouraging any relationship with someone who was your mistress-turned-wife. That is just wrong on so many levels. Please do not ask about my meeting her again. I never want to.

Be blessed

Your friend

My Lost Friend,

First, let me start by apologizing for not adhering to the request to keep my letter to one page in length. I am in a unique position of probably not being here on this earth when this book is published due to my advanced stage of ovarian cancer. I may or may not ever have the opportunity to speak with you again in life, so I want to take this opportunity to tell you what is in my heart and let you know how much I love you and to remind you that life is not promised to anyone. I spent ten years studying to become a doctor to heal others, but sadly I cannot heal myself.

Two years ago, as you know, I was diagnosed with this terrible disease. To say that it was disappointing and truly heartbreaking that you, my friend, never reached out to me is an understatement. I had the love, comfort, and support of your ex-wife and your loving, compassionate children, but from you there was silence.

Five years before the unfolding of your nightmare (that is my personal view), my family and I put everything on hold to attend and celebrate with you and your family that very magical night where you publicly honored you wife of twenty-five years in the most romantic way ever. I am sure you have not forgotten. That was the man that I knew and loved for so many years. I was given the honor of speaking at the occasion.

As I sit here in my bed literally suffering with this horrible disease, I force myself to revisit that night in an attempt to search for some clue of an impending tragedy that I may have missed. There is none. What I did see and hear was the speech that I made. I am including it in my letter as it says everything that I felt then and still do to this day about you, your wife, and children.

Dan, Eva, ladies and gentlemen, good evening. It is my distinct honor to celebrate this wonderful occasion with my dearest friends, Dan and

Eva. I have the unique qualification of having been friends with Dan and Eva. Some people think that I am Dan's friend or Eva's family. I am neither. As a matter of fact, I met Dan at college and I remember he was one of the few guys on campus who I absolutely respected and admired. He constantly talked about Eva and I couldn't wait to meet her. And when I met her I found the sister that I never had. (I am going to get mushy, and I'm sorry.)

We go back many years. I won't be revealing any numbers, but suffice to say it was from the beginning. I have always admired them as a couple and I always admired how romantic Dan is. He never forgets Eva's birthday. He never forgets their anniversary—a quality I pray would rub off on my own husband. (Laughter.)

I have always admired Eva's strength and stamina, and her ability to get it together. No matter what the challenge, no matter what the issue, she is a lady who can get it done. I have the deepest respect and admiration for them.

I love their children as if they were my own and I feel uniquely qualified to say that in my considered opinion if someone had asked Dan, "Tell me how you feel about your wife," he probably would say, "Since the day I found her my heart has wrapped around her and loving her has been a rhapsody." If someone had asked Eva, "How do you feel about your husband?" I am confident, because I know them both very well, Eva would say, "How do I love thee? Let me count the ways. I love you to the depth and breath my soul can reach."

I admire them as a couple because they have shown us that marriage is not just for when the times are great and for when there is laughter, but marriage is for when the times are challenging and when there is pain and when there are tears and when we are not as optimal as we can be.

They have four of the most beautiful, wonderful children. I am trying to pattern my own parenting style from them. I am cheating a little bit. They have my utmost regard and my love.

I would like you all to raise your glasses with me and wish them another fifty years.

Everyone did.

Sadly, just a few short years after that amazing night the nightmare began. You have left everyone who knew you and loved you searching for answers for your unimaginable behavior. You did not divorce your wife, you divorced everyone who has ever known you and loved you. How can this happen? Everyone keeps asking these questions years later. I will shed some light on what I think is the only real explanation.

As a medical doctor, it is my professional opinion and diagnosis that you have a tumor on your frontal lobe. Let me explain. The frontal lobe is responsible for motor function, spontaneity, memory, language, problem solving, initiation, judgment, impulse control, and social and sexual behavior. A brain tumor on the frontal lobe causes behavioral and emotional changes, impaired judgment, memory loss, and reduced mental capacity. Judging from your extreme transformation from a respectable, loving, caring, moral, compassionate person to this uncaring, immoral, detached, wicked individual, I console myself with the fact that my diagnosis is accurate and as a result you cannot be held responsible for the new person that you have become.

Please trust my professional opinion and seek the necessary medical attention so there can be some form of closure for your loved ones, friends, and family.

In closing, I would like to thank you for all the years of friendship. You served many roles in my life. You were my close friend, you were my confidant, you were the brother I never had. When I got married you became close friends with my husband, then you became uncle to my children. You were family.

I pray every day that I would survive this horrible disease. Only a miracle can cure my cancer. I pray every day for that but I am a physician and a realist. It is not going to happen. It is with tear-filled eyes that I end my letter to you. I cry for all my loved ones, friends and family, that I have to leave behind. And I cry you for all the loved ones, friends and family, that you chose to leave behind. I love you.

Your friend,

*Nadine**

---

* Author's note: Nadine passed away four months after writing this letter. Ironically, her memorial service was on the same day as Dan's birthday.